Battle
Normandy 1944:
Life and death in the heat of combat

Battle

Normandy 1944:
Life and death in the heat of combat

Kenneth Macksey

GRUB STREET · LONDON

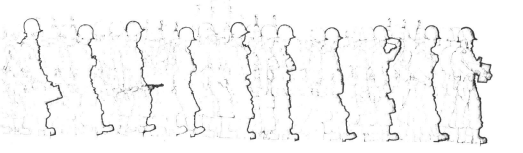

This new edition published by Grub Street
10 Chivalry Road, London SW11 1HT

Copyright © Grub Street 2001
Text copyright © Kenneth Macksey 2001
Cover design Graeme Andrew

The moral right of the author has been asserted

Originally published as *Anatomy of a Battle* by Stein and Day, 1974

British Library Cataloguing in Publication Data
   Macksey, Kenneth, 1923-
   Battle: Normandy 1944: life and death in the heat of combat
   1. World War, 1939-1945 – Campaigns – France – Normandy
   I. Title
   940.5′42142

   ISBN 1 902304 47 0

Printed and bound in Great Britain by
Biddles Ltd, Guildford and King's Lynn

Contents

Acknowledgements

I would like to thank the librarians of the
Ministry of Defence and of the Staff College,
Camberley, in addition to officers of the
Royal School of Artillery for the help they
gave me in assembling material for this book.
I am also grateful to my friends, Ian Hogg,
Robert Cockburn and Dick Colborne, who
contributed their experiences of battle. Many
more besides have spoken to me of fights
long ago; their combined knowledge has
helped clarify my own picture of the
battlefield and brought this book closer to reality.

Illustrations

The front endpaper depicts the view forward
from the position of the 1st Battalion, The
East Hampshire Regiment, prior to their
going into action on 30th July, 1944. The
back endpaper shows diagrammatically the
higher command structure of the British
Army in Normandy and the lower command
structure of the British and American Units
involved in the battle for Vertefeuille Farm
on July 30th. There is a map of the general
situation on the Normandy front on July
20th and July 27th on page 19, and on page
128 a plan of the local situation mid-way
through the battle for Vertefeuille Farm.
Sixteen drawings depicting episodes in the
action appear in the text of the book. All the
illustrations are by Patrick Hargreaves.

Foreword The Combatants

Although it would have served my purpose to concoct an entirely imaginary battle against an anonymous background and sequence of historical events, it seemed important that this narrative should acquire a stronger sense of reality by having a foothold in time. In describing the procedures and analysing the reactions that carry a battalion group into battle I thought it necessary to select the operations of a specified division in an engagement that actually took place. I also felt it essential to eliminate real personalities, except for Commanders-in-Chief, because only in that way could I develop characters and situations to achieve my aim without giving offence to the living or dead. Therefore with the exception of the above all the people and units named in the text are subjects of my own imagination. Any semblance between these imaginary characters and people living or dead is accidental and absolutely unintended.

For example, the operations by the imaginary 1st Battalion, East Hampshire Regiment and imaginary 301st US Battalion, though they take place on the flanks of real formations – 11th Armoured Division and 5th US Infantry Division – during the actual Operation 'Bluecoat', are not about actions performed by the battalions which, on July 30th 1944, carried out similar tasks. Nor are their personalities wittingly known to me. Likewise the staff officers of various formations are fictitious characters, though of course the actual people who filled these appointments are readily identifiable and, in some cases, became distinguished in their profession. My respect for those who fought in Normandy in 11th Armoured Division, among the Americans and their opponents, is sacred and not to be carelessly destroyed by aspersions or invidious comparisons.

Let me add, however, that most incidents are authentic, though drawn from events other than Operation 'Bluecoat'. That is to say, in addition to drawing upon happenings which occurred within my own observation and knowledge, I have carefully studied accounts by authoritative sources in an effort to obtain insight into soldiers' reactions to combat stresses. In particular I have been influenced by two outstanding books on the subject, Lord Moran's *Anatomy of Courage* and Colonel S.L.A. Marshall's *Men against Fire.* The results of their careful analysis of man's performance in battle withstand the test of time.

Glossary

AA & QMG Acting Adjutant and Quartermaster-general. The senior staff officer at a British Divisional Headquarters responsible for matters of personnel and supply.

Adjutant The staff officer at British Battalion Headquarters responsible for operational and personnel matters.

ACV Armoured Command Vehicle. Armoured mobile office, usually equipped with radio.

AFV Armoured Fighting Vehicle, usually a tank or armoured car.

AGRA Army Group Royal Artillery. An assembly of British field, medium and heavy artillery units, grouped for operational and administrative convenience, and switched from front to front in order heavily to reinforce the integral artillery support of lower formations, such as divisions.

ARV Armoured Recovery Vehicle. Specially adapted armoured vehicle (usually a tank with turret removed and winching and lifting gear installed) for use in recovering damaged vehicles in close proximity to the enemy.

ACMO Assistant Counter Mortar Officer. Staff officer usually found at British headquarters, above battalion level, with responsibility for implementing counter-mortar policy between locating devices, headquarters concerned and local artillery units.

ASP As soon as possible.

BAR Browning Automatic Rifle – the light, magazine-fed machine-gun in use with American infantry.

Battalion The basic fighting unit (with a strength of between 600 and 700 men for infantry) to be found in all armies, usually commanded by a lieutenant-colonel or major. Composition was usually specialized i.e. all tank or all infantry, but supplementary weapons, such as mortars and anti-tank guns with infantry, were included. British armoured and artillery units at this level usually were called 'regiments' and are

viii

not to be confused with 'Regiments' in other armies described below.

Battery   A sub-unit of artillery or mortars composed of anything from four to eight guns. Called 'company' in German and US Armies.

BC   Battery Commander.

Bazooka   Short-range rocket-propelled anti-tank weapon of US manufacture.

Bocage   Name given to the Normandy countryside where a system of small fields bounded by double and banked hedges seriously reduced visibility and mobility.

Bofors   A light anti-aircraft gun (40mm calibre) in service with the British Army.

Brigade   Lowest level of 'formation' in British Army, usually consisting of anything from two to five battalions. Usually called 'Regiment' in German and US armies.

Carrier   A light, open-topped armoured tracked vehicle in British Army service, used for various purposes such as the movement of heavy infantry weapons and ammunition, as a mobile command post, or for the evacuation of wounded.

CRA   Commander Royal Artillery. Senior artillery officer working at British divisional level as artillery adviser to the GOC. Usually held the rank of Brigadier.

CO   Commanding Officer of a unit at battalion level.

CCRA   Corps Commander Royal Artillery. CRA's equivalent at Corps Headquarters.

CP   USA Command Post.

Company   A sub-unit of tanks, infantry (fighting strength about 100) or artillery (see battery above). Called 'Squadron' in British armoured units.

CSM   Company Sergeant-major. The senior non-commissioned officer in a British company.

Corps   A higher formation employed to command a variable number of divisions and attached formations such as AGRAs.

CB   Counter Bombardment. The organization and system deployed to attack enemy guns and mortars.

Crocodile   A British Churchill-type tank, fitted as a flame-thrower and towing its flame fuel and pressure bottles in an armoured trailer.

DCBO   Divisional Counter Bombardment Officer. The artillery staff officer responsible for implementing counter-bombardment policy.

DF   Defensive fire. Term denoting the system adopted by artillery and mortars for laying down pre-determined fire in protection of a defended locality.

Division   The lowest level of command to combine every part of an army's fighting and administrative elements. Usually consisted of two or more brigades plus several tank, artillery and engineer units, along with administrative units for supply and medical care, etc.

Exec   Executive Officer. Senior officer at US Army battalion level. Roughly equivalent to Second-in-Command of a British battalion.

Firefly   British modification of the standard Sherman tank by the substitution of the much more powerful, long 17-pounder gun for the 75mm gun originally fitted.

Flail   British modification of the standard Sherman tank by the addition of a powered rotating drum, with chains attached, to beat the ground ahead with the intention of exploding mines.

FDL   Forward Defended Locality. The equivalent of the frontal firing line of battle.

FOO   Forward Observation Officer. British term denoting an artillery officer, located near the front line, tasked to locate enemy targets and direct fire wherever required.

FUP   Forming up place. A tactical attack location, out of enemy view if possible, in which troops assemble immediately prior to advancing into contact with the enemy. A British term.

GOC   General Officer Commanding a British division – normally a Major-General.

GSO   General Staff Officer. Found by various grades and ranks in the planning, operational, intelligence and co-ordinating branches of formations at all levels.

H hour	Term used as datum in setting a time for action. Thus if H hour is 1000 hrs, H minus 10 is 0950 hrs.
Hauptfeldwebel	The senior non-commissioned officer in a German infantry battalion. Roughly equivalent to a Regimental Sergeant-major (RSM) in the British Army and a 1st Sergeant in the US Army.
IO	Intelligence officer employed to seek, interpret, synthesize and distribute information about the enemy.
Jagdpanther	German self-propelled anti-tank gun with very thick, sloped armour and a long, high-velocity 88mm gun.
Jeep	Small four-wheel drive vehicle of US manufacture in general use throughout the US and British armies.
LST	Landing Ship Tank. A sea-going vessel used to transport tanks and, if necessary, unload them through a bow-ramp direct to beaches.
LMG	Light machine-gun.
MP	British Military Policeman.
Mortàr	Light weapon for firing projectiles through high angles so as to throw intensive plunging fire upon the enemy. Range up to about 3,000 metres for 81mm versions.
Nebelwerfer	German six-barrelled weapon firing rocket-propelled projectiles out to above 7,000 metres. Celebrated for the sighing sound of its projectiles which won it the name 'Moaning Minnie'.
Net	British shortened version for 'radio network' – a grouping of radio stations operating on the same frequency.
O Group	Orders Group. Term in British use to describe an assembly of leaders to receive orders.
Oberfeldwebel	A non-commissioned officer in the German Army, one rank below Hauptfeldwebel (see above).
Obergefreiter	A corporal in the German Army.
Panzerfaust	German equivalent of the US bazooka.
PIAT	Projector Infantry Anti-Tank. A light infantry weapon in use with the British Army for throwing

	a hollow-charge anti-tank grenade a distance of about 100 yards.
Platoon	Small infantry sub-unit usually consisting of about thirty men led by a junior officer.
R Group	Reconnaissance Group. Term in British use to describe a small assembly of leaders engaged upon pre-battle reconnaissance.
Regiment	Lowest level of 'formation' in German and US Armies usually comprising anything from two to five battalions. Usually called 'Brigade' in the British Army.
RSM	Regimental Sergeant-major. Senior non-commissioned officer in a British battalion or regiment.
RV	Rendezvous.
Sappers	British title for field engineers.
SP	Self-propelled. Usually used in relation to a self-propelled gun. The Jagdpanther described above was an example, being similar to a tank except that the main armament had a limited traverse instead of being mounted in a fully traversing turret.
SS	Schutz Staffeln. Elite troops of the German forces celebrated for their fighting efficiency and ruthlessness.
Sheldrake	British Army security term used to denote the senior artillery officer on a radio network.
SDS	Special Dispatch Service.
Snowdrop	Slang for a US Army Military Policeman.
Stonk	Artillery term in British Army use to describe a linear concentration of shell-fire. Misused by the uninitiated to describe almost any type of artillery concentrated fire.
Sunray	British Army security term used to denote the commander of a radio network station.
Troop	Lowest organization in a tank or artillery unit, usually comprising four tanks or four guns.
Uncle Target	The concerted fire of all the guns under command of a British division.
Victor Target	The concerted fire of all the guns under command of a British corps.
Warrant Officer	Senior non-commissioned officer. In the British Army a Sergeant-major.

1 The Warning Order

The white SDS label covering the buff-coloured envelope was marked 'Secret' because the envelope's contents, if known to the German enemy, would compromise the lives of thousands of British and American soldiers. The words 'Op Immediate', also printed on the label, meant that its priority of dispatch was most urgent. All this was necessary because the typed Signal Message Form carried a formal Warning Order calling men to battle at short notice.

It lay in the pouch of Lance-Corporal Charlie Barker of the Royal Corps of Signals who was taking it to Headquarters, 11th Armoured Division – briefly described on the label, in the official military Staff Duties' abbreviation, as 'Main 11th Armd Div'. Neither Barker nor his jeep driver, Fred Riley, knew the envelope's contents, only that they must find their way down two miles of dusty, narrow Normandy lanes from the Headquarters of the Second Army to the HQ of the armoured division, thread their way through the endless convoys of lorries moving between the combat and rear areas, and deliver it to the division without delay. That was easy. Riley had been there twice before and hardly needed to spot the headquarters' traffic sign – a white figure '40' on a small, black background with its arrow pointing through a gateway into an orchard. They approached the red-capped military policeman, who waved them on, and drew up outside the clerks' office truck which stood alongside a high hedge, merged by camouflage nets with this typical feature of the dense Normandy *bocage*.

1

Barker handed the envelope to the corporal clerk whose desk stood at the top of the steps leading into the truck, and waited until the receipt had been signed. Without opening the envelope the corporal registered its arrival and then took it to the Chief Clerk, WO II Cutler, who was seated at the back of the office. Cutler was the only clerk on duty with authority to open 'Secret' documents and he was already awaiting its arrival. A friend at Corps had warned him by telephone and not long ago the General had departed for Corps headquarters in something of a hurry. These were usually the first indications that something important was afoot. He ripped open the envelope, pulled out the message form and scanned its contents, stood up and then paused to give instructions to the corporal. 'It's a Warning Order to move today,' he said. 'Usual drill, Corporal Derbyshire. Shake out all the duty clerks and begin the routine. Clear typewriters and duplicating machines – and this time see they're a lot cleaner than they were before "Goodwood". Give Signals a buzz, too, and tell them what's brewing. It'll shake 'em. They're away at baths mostly I think! OK? I'm off with this to Major Sykes.'

Walking under fruit trees, with their clusters of little hard green cider apples, Cutler made for a tent whose occupant was seated at a table writing a letter. From somewhere to the southward he heard the rumble of guns. Apart from that, he ruminated, and the never-ending roar of vehicles passing along the nearby lane it was difficult, for the moment, to believe they were at war.

For Arthur Sykes, the GSO 2 of 11th Armoured Division, this, too, was a rare moment of repose, and the first time since he had landed in Normandy over a month ago in which he had tried to reflect upon the battle to Ellen. When writing his daily letter from the assembly camps in England, from the ship in mid-Channel and thereafter in random spare moments between spells of duty, he had spared her the war's uglier details, preferring to concentrate upon describing the people he met and the countryside he saw. But on this day, 28th July, he somehow felt changed and dissatisfied, indefinably unlike the man who, on 13th June, full of curiosity and apprehension, had stepped ashore in France. Then he had been full of confidence in his fitness for combat after four years' training. Now the campaign and battle had taken him in thrall and converted him into an automaton which served a juggernaut. This letter, therefore, was an exercise in escapism, an attempt to recover his sense of individuality. It was a way, too, of unburdening his dissatisfaction.

He saw the Chief Clerk approaching and guessed the portent of the message form. Doggedly he read the letter's final paragraph again.

'You may ask,' he had written, 'how it is that the officers and men keep going when under such duress as I have described. I cannot pretend to have the answer to such a complex question, for it is deeply wrapped in psychology of which, as you charmingly say, I know so little. I merely receive and pass orders, trying to reduce violent things to routine in a crazy world, well knowing that, as a staff officer, I am somewhat divorced from reality. For a start I am far less at risk than the fighting men, who comply with their orders. I do my best to avoid taking risks and just work hard, most of the time (you'll be surprised to learn), while they live and work in greater squalor and far more fear of their lives. They are trained and they obey. Hobo, the man who formed this division, reckoned that you conquered fear by way of frequent contact with it. He was - is - an unusual man and holds views (of which that is one) with which I disagree. I somehow think that allowance must be made for this in the framing of a battle plan. Not my responsibility, thank God, but it cannot be ignored.'

He glanced at the Chief Clerk standing impatiently beside him, asked him to sit down and carefully finished the letter. 'Nemesis, in the shape of Mr Cutler, has arrived, clutching a piece of paper which, unless I'm a Dutchman, sends us on our travels again.' He suppressed a flicker of annoyance at the unknown person who seemed set upon disrupting his communion with a young wife he had married only three months ago and of whom he knew far too little. Firmly he wrote the words of adoration, which frequent repetition was already beginning to stereotype, and signed off. Prising open the flap of an envelope that was already tacky from exposure to the damp atmosphere, he closed the letter.

'First things first, Mr Cutler,' he remarked with a smile. He read the signal and allowed the army machine to enmesh him again. Then he sketched brief notes on his millboard pad, rapidly converting the contents of the Warning Order into an outline summary of the operation it foreshadowed – the semblance of the Warning Order which he, too, would soon issue to 11th Armoured Division. Composed again in mind, shackled once more to the staff officer's strict routine, he picked up the signal and walked to ACV 5 where the GSO 1, Lieutenant-Colonel Stuart Pocock, was working.

Staff officers are trained to think logically, even to criticize at the right time and place, and yet to suppress emotion and concentrate coolly upon translating their commander's thoughts and demands (even the most confused of them from the heat of battle) into select, precise phrases that can readily be understood by frightened men with the minimum of mental effort. The Staff turns crude ideas into refined execution – or so they had taught Sykes at the Staff College: six weeks of war had broadened that education, demonstrating the validity of Staff College theory, emphasizing that military pedantry has its uses in instilling confidence by overcoming, through standardized procedure, the chances of error. Error had been minimized, he found, by the meticulous employment of the recognized drills which reduced communication to a common denominator. Moreover pride in flat 'staff duties', as they were called, actually seemed to generate the great dynamism. Therefore his treatment of this Warning Order would be a studied attempt at greater economy than ever before.

The sequence of formal orders began at Headquarters, Second British Army, and was repeated to its various corps, in addition to several other divisions, besides 11th Armoured. Here, in writing, was a hint of what the General must be learning from HQ VIII Corps:

1. VIII and XXX Corps will attack southward from area Caumont Noyers.
2. No move from present locations before 282000 hours.

3. Block Timings follow ASP. Routes to new Assembly Area as at attached trace.
4. Advance parties to RV with XXX Corps reps in Caumont by 290600 hours.
5. Administrative Instructions . . .

and there followed a few more terse lines which detailed the preliminary arrangements for the repositioning of supplies and transport, above all the movement of artillery ammunition to satisfy the guns' needs.

By studying the map Pocock conjured up in his imagination what the text left unsaid. The division was to move westward and soon - starting in fact before midnight - to take up an attack position near Caumont. The journey might be only twenty-five miles, but it was along narrow roads of fragile foundation that wound across the grain of main supply routes which sustained the front line units from the maintenance base areas near the coast. 'Even if this move didn't begin before dawn tomorrow,' said Pocock, 'we'd be hard-pressed to prepare and dispatch full instructions in time for the entire division to assemble, and to organize adequate traffic control. Yet it looks as if Army intends us to move tonight.' Pocock ran his eye over the situation map displayed behind talc on ACV 5's wall, turning its symbols and the information at his disposal into a mental projection of the future. Although it was obvious that a major regrouping of Second Army was intended, it was also clear, because his GOC had been called to VIII Corps, that the division remained under that Corps' command. At this moment, however, Caumont lay in XXX Corps' sector, adjacent to American First Army. Therefore, VIII Corps was about to be squeezed into XXX Corps - perhaps even among the Americans - and that, presumably, demanded a wholesale reshuffle of troops throughout the Army sector. The operational theatre was expanding southward fast where long, blue, chinagraphed arrows showed the American thrust lengthening past St Lo towards Brittany.

'You know what this means?' he asked Sykes. 'That's the

thickest bit of *bocage* in Normandy. God knows how we'll manage.' But the tactical problems he swiftly dismissed in favour of a brief re-analysis of the state of the division itself. Was it equal to yet another severe test coming so hard upon the last which had been its most damaging? How might he advise his General if that question were asked?

For five days 11th Armoured Division had been recuperating from the hammering it had received during Operation 'Goodwood'. To the south of Caen lay the corpses of so many of its best men, those who had learnt their craft in England in the course of three years' training. Their place was now being filled by untried reinforcements to be absorbed among the survivors who sat back, momentarily, in contemplation of the shock of a gruelling battle. The first-fruits of this breathing space for the division lay typed on Arthur Sykes's desk – an outline scheme for their future grouping in battle. 'In this thick country,' had declared the GOC at a conference of senior commanders, 'we must never again allow the armour to become segregated, grouped all in one block with a dribble of infantry support while, two fields distant, the Infantry Brigade is stuck fast for lack of tanks. We must balance tanks and infantry – give half of each, if necessary, to each brigade so they can respond independently to any situation.' The discussion had expanded in harmony upon this theme, each brigade commander adding his opinions and experience until a reshaped division emerged. As a result, commanders and men would be more sensitive and less dogmatic in their outlook, prepared to react flexibly with swift reapportioning of the striking force of tanks, artillery or infantry to any one of the brigades to the slightest change in terrain or enemy backlash. 'All yours, Stuart,' the GOC had said making quickly for the door as they finished. 'Put it on paper so everybody will know what gives next time. I'm off for a look at the night-fighting experiment.' So Pocock and Sykes, along with Charles Dyer, the AA and QMG, had put in two days' grafting work – amending the Standing Orders, reorganizing the supply arrangements, resetting Staff Tables and adjusting operational procedures so that, whatever demands the GOC might throw upon them in deploying and redeploying the mixed elements of the formation in battle, they could rapidly formulate radioed instructions that everybody would understand and implement at a moment's notice. 'Training,' as the GOC remarked when they finally explained their schemes to him, 'never ends. I like this. See everybody's told all about it too. If there's time we'll run a short exercise for commanders and staffs.'

To Sykes, as GSO 2, fell the task of dissemination to brigade staff officers lower down the chain of command. Meantime Pocock spent a day visiting units where they lay hidden in the orchards, woods and fields of the surrounding Norman countryside taking advantage of an opportunity to speak informally to officers and men for the first time since their arrival in France in June. He had tried to measure the effects of the transformation from training to practice. He also wanted to meet the replacements. Yet it came as a surprise to find so many of the old faces remaining. The daily sequence of casualty reports, with their sorry tale of heavy losses to the south of Caen, had appalled him, the post-battle sight of wrecked machines packed within a few acres of cornfield had been a shock. Nevertheless, with 1st Pentland Yeomanry he found the Commanding Officer, Lieutenant-Colonel Douglas Ferriers, talking lightheartedly to a majority of the original squadron commanders – with one exception, in fact, all of those who crossed the Channel a month ago.

'Good of you to look in, Stuart,' greeted Ferriers. 'I think you know everybody? Or had you met Philip Snow before? He's taken over A Squadron since Adrian went last week. Have some of this bloody awful compo tea. Or would you rather something stronger?'

'Just tea, thanks, I'm visiting the East Hampshires next and have to beware Edward Simcox,' he replied amid laughter. 'Yes, of course I remember Philip. You nearly ran me over driving aboard the LST – my fault too. I was sorry to hear about Adrian.'

'Thank you, sir,' said Snow, his attention distracted momentarily from the visitor. He was trying to forget Adrian but now, once more, he was reminded of his friend leaping from the disabled tank, the sight of dust spurting as the German machine-gunner loosed-off, and of his squadron commander falling out of view into a bed of nettles.

They drank from china mugs and conversed. 'Would you care to look round?' asked Ferriers at last. 'Philip would be pleased to display his new command. Don't worry if he's not used to being called major!'

They gulped the unpalatable fluid which masqueraded as tea and walked round the edge of the field into the adjoining orchard where Sherman tanks, draped in camouflage nets and hung with bivouacs, lay close alongside the steep hedgerow banks. Generators' throb and the whiff of petrol and exhaust fumes tainted the atmosphere. Crews tended their machines. Those with tanks which still blatantly displayed the Black Bull divisional sign demonstrated they had belonged to the unit in England; those innocent of heraldic paint advertised a recent arrival from the Tank Delivery Squadron near Bayeux, to replace a casualty.

'Up to strength again, Philip?' asked Pocock.

'Last one came in last night. We lost less than B or C and consequently I've had to make fewer readjustments within the troops. One troop lost two out of three but the rest only one apiece. The replacements don't seem a bad lot – some of them were in the squadron back in England.'

'I remember that sergeant over there,' said Pocock. 'Gave me a cup of tea down on the Hard.'

Sergeant Angus Grant, a pre-war Territorial soldier and car salesman who had acquired the veneer of a pre-war regular, was supervising track tensioning on a Sherman, adding his weight to the extension bar when required.

'Good to see you again,' said Pocock as he and the troop sergeant exchanged salutes. 'A new one? What happened to the last?'

'Stopped an eighty-eight, sir,' replied Grant in gentle Highland accent. 'She brewed slow but we lost our kit – and all the beer too.'

'Lost his co-driver, too,' added Philip.

'Aye, a good lad young Pat, but they say he'll be alright. Just a nick in his backside as he ran for it when we bailed out. Pity.

He was a fine cook and this new chappie, Armstrong, seems barely capable of working the cooker let alone boiling the water. Still, he can drive - I'll gie him that, brought this 'un in yesterday fine.'

Armstrong sat crouched in solitude by the side of the bivouac, pumping a pressure cooker that gurgled with the intermittent splutter which indicated a sticking needle-valve and the prospect for the crew of a late lunch. He did not look up for, as yet, he felt like a foreigner press-ganged into a close-gathered clan. From within the turret came the sound of Glenn Miller's band relayed through the tank radio headsets, and the clink of metal upon metal where the gunner, Benstead, helped by McAteer, the radio operator, was reassembling the 75mm gun's breach after cleaning. Two legs, protruding above the engine compartment, showed where Brown, the driver, was checking an oil-filter leak. This crew would not readily admit that a tank, so recently delivered from Base, could be the mechanical equal of the one they had previously tended with such care - which now stood a gutted, discoloured wreck, beyond recovery except as scrap metal, upon the slope of Bourguebus Ridge.

Pocock had departed from the Yeomanry, pleased that this armoured regiment seemed little the worse for its experience - might, in fact, have benefited from it. He had rediscovered the old zeal and sensed a growing maturity among tank crews, all of whom had seen and felt the shock of war and now understood the difference between training exercises' pretence and battle's reality. He guessed they might all the better calculate a risk and balance it against the essential demands of survival, perhaps achieving greater results at a lower cost. Would they in future, however, hesitate and blunt their élan when under the fire of a professional enemy of such quality as the German Panzer Divisions they had been fighting? It was their crews' respect for enemy prowess that, perhaps, gave cause for disquiet, their grim understanding in July of a technical inequality they had not suspected in May. It had been frankly stated by Lieutenant Andrew Partridge, one of Snow's troop leaders: 'You could see the bloody Panthers and Tigers up on the crest and we were hitting them dead centre; but our stuff just bounced off! Theirs

didn't though. Every time a coconut. We're outclassed! Only the
Fireflies, with their 17-pounders, ruffle them, but what good's
one in five in a squadron? There just aren't enough!' Pocock
suspected hysteria in the outburst but restrained himself, for the
cry was common and, partly, the by-product of public discussion
in parliament and in the press. British tank crews were entering
battle all too aware of their technical deficiencies and, in some
units, notably those which had seen hard fighting in the desert
and Italy, were getting a reputation for being battle shy.

They looked at matters from a different angle in the 1st
Battalion, the East Hampshire Regiment – as befitted an
unarmoured infantry battalion that crouched near the ground and
was, inherently, prey to every battlefield weapon. Over the
whisky deprived of water that Pocock knew, from experience,
Edward Simcox would thrust into his hand, came that
Lieutenant-colonel's listing of infantry woes. 'It's not their tanks
that worry us, though God knows they're tiresome. We can hold
them in *bocage*, such as we found round Gavrus, because the
17-pounders in the anti-tank regiment polish them off when our
tanks aren't around. Even our own 6-pounders score except
against the front of a Panther. No, what's hurting us are mortars
and those fiendish Nebelwerfers.'

They had been joined by B Company Commander, Major
David Garston, and the Battalion Medical Officer, Felix
Chandler. 'Seven out of ten of my cases are mortar wounds and
pretty ugly too,' explained Chandler. 'Bits ripped off all over the
place. There was one chap the other day . . .'

'OK, Doc, spare us,' cut in Garston. 'It's true enough, though.
They put down concentrations so damn quick and pull out so
smart our own gunners seem unable to catch 'em. The BC was
telling me only yesterday they're off before there's a chance of
counter-battery fire catching up. Our chaps'll take a chance
against a tank or even a machine-gun – something they feel they
can swipe. But these bloody mortars are another matter. There's
no hitting back. It's the devil to get the men up and going once
the Hun puts down a DF. I had the sod of a job getting them
moving towards Hubert Folie, though once we got there it wasn't
too bad.'

'You should travel in a tank,' suggested Pocock.

'What, and fry like all those poor bastards in 29th Armoured last week?' asked Simcox. 'Have another whisky!'

Officers were drifting into the mess tent at lunchtime, talking quietly among themselves, picking up London newspapers – three days old – or settling down to take their turn censoring letters from the pile that the soldiers replenished with unbridled industry. The infantry privates had particular difficulty in finding an opportunity to write home – no tank or lorry as shelter for them in time of action, but instead a shallow slit-trench which gave little protection from the rain. Put them in a tent with pen and paper and they unburdened pent-up feelings upon their families – and their officers. Yet, like Sykes, for fear of distressing their families, they were usually careful to conceal, in addition to military secrets, their innermost dreads and uncertainties. The man who gave way to an hysterical outburst was at once suspect and watched more carefully by a diligent officer. A conversation piece between subaltern censors reached Pocock:

'I do wish Charlie Morris would exclude me from the dialogue. Here it is again – in brackets – "That OK with you Mr Davis?" '

'Rate yourself lucky you don't have to read Ingram's round-by-round reminiscence of embarkation leave with his new wife,' replied another. 'The things they did! It fair makes the hair curl my dear.'

'And rouses your jealousy? Well, BURMA, as they now seem to say, instead of SWALK.'

Pocock could no longer refrain from asking a question.

'I'm sorry,' he said, 'but I could not help overhearing. I was brought up on Sealed With A Loving Kiss – if that's your interpretation of SWALK. But BURMA is a new one on me?'

'Be Undressed Ready My Angel,' promptly replied Lieutenant Frank Davis, 'though there are some who substitute "upstairs" for "undressed". It's a matter of taste, sir.'

From an adjacent orchard came the sounds of a company being called to the cookhouse. Pocock watched them pass – boisterous, tanned and fit – cleaner, too, since he last watched them grim-faced and caked in dust, moving at measured pace

towards the tank battle's turmoil. That morning they had bathed
at the mobile bath unit and received a change of underclothes.
Cinema-shows had been arranged for the evening entertainment
and, for some, a visit to the rest camp by the coast where, for a
couple of days, they could shed their apprehension. He knew that
if he visited their bivouac area he would find weapons cleaned
and oiled, magazines carefully recharged – and slit trenches in
profusion, ready for occupation when the German air force paid
its nightly visit. On exercises in England it had been asking the
impossible to make them dig deeply; now they did so with an
abandon that knew no limits. Yet, as Pocock correctly guessed,
they would visit the local village as smartly dressed as once they
were at Aldershot prior to embarkation for Normandy.
Everywhere he was meticulously saluted. Here, in accord with
his conditioned judgement of military values, he found an
essential discipline, the sort that was cast in careful training and
which survived the losses and strains of battle.

Had it been possible he would have toured one of the field
artillery regiments, too, but the Gunners remained committed to
action at the front, supporting another formation even though
their own division had been withdrawn for a rest. It seemed like
a mark of ingratitude for services that had been well rendered,
for it had been the Gunners' ability to produce quick concentrations of fire at almost any time and point which frequently
prevented the infantry from being overborne and which
immensely aided the tanks by neutralizing enemy anti-tank guns.
Tanks might look omnipotent and massed aerial bombing, such
as they had witnessed, seemed fearfully impressive. Yet, Pocock
reflected, it was the Gunners who had most frequently saved
them all and, fortunately, at small cost to themselves in casualties. Along the road he had met Brian Culpepper, 'P' Battery
commander in 203rd Field Regiment, and Brian said they were
hoping for relief in twenty-four hours. The Gunner Major's jeep
driver had used the Royal Artillery's motto when he voiced his
comrades' thoughts: 'Ubique – the whole ruddy time'.

Sykes interrupted Pocock's reverie.

'I've drafted a Warning Order, sir,' he said, holding out the message form, 'and you'll see I've called the Commander's O Group for 2100 hours. He was on the phone a moment back. That's what he wants.'

Pocock read the message which was roughly similar in content to the one already received from Second Army. Beyond the ACV door he observed the chief clerk, hovering and eager to seize the message, once it had been signed, to begin the process of distribution to the entire division. His clerks were ready, duplicating machinery cleared of inessential matter, envelopes addressed, Acknowledgements Register prepared. Standing by, too, were the dispatch riders, briefed as to which unit locations the order was to be taken.

'Did the GOC say when he'd be back, Arthur?'

'Said he was on his way. He'll be here any moment. Do you want to hold the Warning Order 'til you've seen him?'

'Well, I'd like to be sure he doesn't want to say anything specific about what grouping we'll adopt. You see, he might want to regroup here rather than in the new Assembly Area, 'specially if there's not much time and if this move's going to be as complex as I suspect. What d'you think?'

They were still discussing the problem when the GOC's jeep drove up. He entered, compact and alert, one of the most battle-hardened tank leaders in the British Army - a man whose experience of war had been tempered in the desert and quenched by the ravages of defeat as much as forged in the satisfaction of victory. One who instinctively realized, better than any of them, how minutes saved by a quick decision could save hours and perhaps days in battle, dramatically swinging the outcome one way or the other. He listened to Pocock's question and immediately replied:

'It's simply a matter of how quickly we can send the Movement Order and when we move. As yet there's no firm time of departure nor time for attack. But we're being pushed into the closest of country, so it might be better to sort out into our fighting groups before we get there. Here, Stuart, these are the groupings I worked out on the way back from Corps. Let's move in that order, so attach 'em to the Warning Order. Come and see me as soon as you're finished. It'll be a busy night.'

2　Debate among Commanders-in-Chief

In conflicts between nations, whether in the spacious upper levels of Army Commands or in the lowest huddle of an infantry section's water-logged foxhole, issues are decided by the most efficient possible combinations among small fighting groups. Teams under an appointed leader, each member directed to his allocated task, or working spontaneously in unison at the demands of emergency, are the arbiters of decision. The strongest team usually wins. At the pinnacle of power Commanders-in-Chief scheme among themselves, sifting evidence, evaluating political stresses, calculating logistics with subordinates and staffs, evolving the gigantic strategic combinations and manoeuvres, dispatching ice-cold orders until they finally point the lowliest infantryman in the enemy's direction, there to fight the squalid, tactical engagement. But most people retain independence of mind and inclinations of their own: some accept orders without demur but as many more have to be persuaded to risk their lives.

When the Anglo-American Armies crossed the beaches of Normandy on June 6th 1944, they came to France in response to provocation by the Germans and at the desire of peoples expressed through their leaders' persuasions and directives as matters of National Policy. They were dedicated to a fight to the finish because propaganda, which simulated grievances where, sometimes, none existed, and stimulated enthusiasm when it flagged, implied there was no alternative.

14

Britain, since her ejection from France in 1940 by the conquering German Army, had acquired as the emotive mainspring of her policy (instigated by the stark demands of survival) the desire to return and reconquer. For America the issue was less distinctly defined. Nevertheless the moment she became embroiled in war in 1941 she reached agreement with the British that the subjugation of Germany should be completed before that of Japan – even though it was Japan by her attack upon Pearl Harbor which had finally impelled the Americans to take up arms. From these fundamental political reactions to challenges of force stemmed the chain reaction of Grand Strategy which reached completion at the strategic arrival of Allied troops to fight the tactical battle among Normandy's hedgerows.

The shaping of a politico-military policy between allies is never a simple, one-shot process. Though President Roosevelt and Prime Minister Churchill had given their personal approval to an agreed Grand Strategy, constantly shifting pressures persisted in the lower realms of power to alter strategic emphasis, sometimes resulting in attempts to cause an inversion of the original, central theme. Within the theme would be played variations in the movement of ships, aircraft, war material and men to overcome unforeseen threats and take advantage of fortuitous opportunities. Successful higher policies depend, however, upon long-term consistency of aim. The Germans had dissipated their original energies because they made fundamental changes in their Grand Strategy: the Allies did better because they tended to persevere, despite the temptations to alter their direction under the pressures of myriad different opinions and emotions.

Towards the end of 1943 formidable forces had been positively allocated to an invasion of France and were assembling in the USA and Britain. The Allied Cs-in-C were formulating their ideas for a campaign designed totally to defeat the German nation. Their strategic and tactical plans were based upon the availability of a massive amount of information and data to make the most efficient use of enormous material and manpower strength. By calculation they endeavoured to reduce error and waste; by a studied abstention from national bias they tried to achieve unanimity in a common purpose. They developed excellent communications between different nationalities at all levels of command: common failure threatened only when these communications faltered. To some of the planners, particularly among the Americans, this supreme operation of war almost amounted to a gigantic engineering project which subjugated human relations.

The threat of an imminent invasion was well recognized by the Germans in late 1943 and preparations to defeat it sharply increased. Under an authoritarian organization such as theirs, dictated by the Reich Chancellor and Supreme Commander, Adolf Hitler, complete unity of purpose might have been expected. In theory one man's word was law. Centralized planning tended to overrule time-consuming consultation. And yet there was disarray in the ranks, for while Hitler retained an ostensibly detailed and inhibiting remote control of operations, there was no agreement about strategy among the Army leadership. Field-Marshal Gerd von Rundstedt, the C-in-C West, had postulated a classic, flexible defence based on his personal experience of mobile warfare, which, in 1940 and 1941, had suffered little interference from hostile air forces. But, since 1942, the commander of his Army Group 'B', Field-Marshal Erwin Rommel, had gained harsh experience of the effects of persistent, heavy air attacks upon his lines of supply and front-line troops. He considered, therefore, that mobile defence would be impossible: the invasion would have to be stopped on the beaches and defeated there. The Germans eventually adopted a strategy which fell between the two extremes, with Hitler, habitually defying suggestions that involved the surrender of conquered territory, dictating a policy designed to rope off the Allied beachhead as it took shape after the invasion.

Unity of Allied military purpose was assured when their Supreme Commander, General Dwight Eisenhower, handed operational control of the invasion forces to the C-in-C of the British 21st Army Group, General Sir Bernard Montgomery. It was he who formulated local strategy, loftily explaining its subsequent developments to his Supreme Commander and his Staff. His initial objectives were mandatory: to seize as wide a bridgehead as possible between the River Orne and the Cotentin peninsula. A complementary aim was also demanded if the essential breakout towards central France was to be eased – 'to peg out claims' as far as possible inland. The essential feature of the Montgomery strategy was psychological. He wanted the Germans to think, as a result of repeated attacks against the eastern flank, that he intended to break out through the open country near Caen when, in fact, he meant only to attract German strength in that direction while actually disrupting a weakened opponent in the difficult, enclosed country on the western flank. Throughout June and most of July, while the Normandy lodgement was consolidated and fresh resources brought in by sea, British Second Army, under General Sir Miles Dempsey, fought bitter and costly battles to pin the bulk of the German Army – particularly its armoured formations – close to the environs of Caen. Simultaneously the US First Army, under General Omar Bradley, strove hard to clear the western flank, including the port of Cherbourg, and unobtrusively assemble massive forces for an offensive south of St Lo.

By July 18th the climax to this strategy had been reached. That day Second Army launched Operation 'Goodwood' – a mighty heave by three armoured and four infantry divisions southward from Caen towards Falaise, its aim, as stated in Montgomery's written instructions, in confirmation of his verbal orders, 'To engage the German armour in battle and "write it down" to such an extent that it is of no further value. . .' Two days later was to come First Army's contribution, the main thrust against a weakened enemy by three armoured and eight infantry divisions in an operation called 'Cobra'. And then things went wrong for the Allies. The British armoured forces in Operation 'Goodwood' ran headlong into an ambush prepared by the very German armoured forces they had set out to 'write down'. They had succeeded in magnetizing the Germans to the eastern flank, leaving just two Panzer Divisions facing First Army, but their losses in tanks were far heavier than those of the Germans. Then, on July 20th, when First Army was due to start, the already bad weather deteriorated: Operation 'Cobra' had to be postponed.

Five days were to elapse before 'Cobra' could begin: a time

fraught with the peril that the Germans might restore their pre-Goodwood posture and re-position stronger forces opposite the Americans. Five days of worry, when pressure from 'Goodwood' died away and the Allied commanders, tense with anxiety, whiled away the time debating the theme of Montgomery's strategy. Eisenhower seemed to have gathered the notion that, since 'Goodwood' had failed to make extensive ground and suffered such losses, the prospects of 'Cobra' succeeding in the enclosed ground on the westward flank had withered. He was harried by adverse press comments and encouraged in his doubts by his Deputy, Air-Marshal Sir Arthur Tedder, who, far from supporting Montgomery, chose this depressing moment to suggest a radical change of strategy. Tedder expressed concern that the *bocage* country in the west – small fields bounded by thick hedges, steeply banked – was no place for unrestricted movement such as First Army would need in order to achieve the principal breakout. His intervention smacked of intrigue, but was far from the first instance of its kind in history. Commanders are a jealous bunch. In response, of course, Montgomery had no alternative but to maintain his original course, not only in the confidence of his own judgement, but because a change at that juncture, when the troops were virtually formed up for battle and waiting only for good weather, would cancel out all previous efforts which led up to this opportunity. As the criticism mounted he was supported in his resolution by Bradley with 'we must just grin and bear it' – good advice for strategists when their schemes are under attack by the uninitiated. Montgomery might have suffered less criticism, however, had he taken greater care to ensure his Supreme Commander's thorough understanding of the plan – but Montgomery, victor in many fields, rather despised his master's military competence, for Eisenhower had no battle laurels to his credit. Montgomery would have been better advised to make less sweeping claims to the press about the prospects for 'Goodwood' – as he later was to admit – but Montgomery was as eager for glory as the next man, and convinced of the necessity for propaganda assistance. There had been failure of communications all round at the highest level, partly because no set drill existed for consultations between the principals. They met and corresponded only irregularly and, mostly, informally. Thus they indulged in a less rigorous and disciplined relationship than that which existed, as of strict routine, between the commanders and staffs of lower formations - the HQs of corps, divisions, brigades, and their subordinate units.

The discord between deities at once became academic when 'Cobra' began brilliantly and, in a rush, burst through the thin German defences. The Americans headed rapidly for Avranches, driving a shattered enemy before them. Near Caen, however, the stalemate persisted when diversionary attacks ran foul of the same fierce and unyielding opposition as had smothered 'Goodwood'. The British Second Army stood immobilized and unemployed when all else was in motion. It is a sound military principle to draw back from failure and reinforce success. This Montgomery now did.

On July 27th the Americans had reached a point midway between St Lo and Avranches and their offensive was rapidly gathering speed and threat. Thus far they had been opposed only

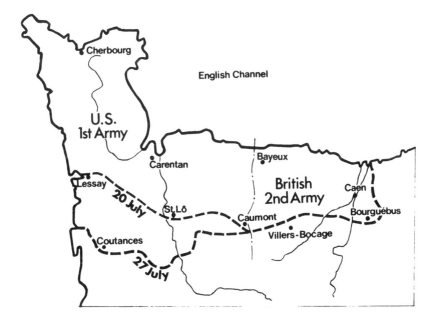

by scattered German infantry and two Panzer Divisions, for the other six Panzer Divisions intently watched the British at Caen. It could hardly last of course. Soon the tanks of these Panzer Divisions must redeploy westward in an attempt to constrict the American progress. Consequently it became desirable for the Allies to widen the breadth of penetration in the American sector and increase its base as well as pace of advance, automatically distracting the Germans, who were already concentrating against the initial incursion, compelling them to spread their counter-blows over a wider area. Montgomery conferred with his Army commanders that morning and gave verbal instructions to the Second Army (later confirmed in writing) to strike south from Caumont – that is, to the east of the existing American pene-tration into a zone as yet lightly held by the Germans. Six divisions were to be used 'and the sooner it begins the better'. In leisurely style Dempsey contemplated starting on August 2nd, but Eisenhower, seeing Montgomery's instruction next day, chimed in to give added volition. 'I feel very strongly that a three-division attack *now* on Second Army's right flank will be worth more than six-division attack in five days' time,' he signalled. It was timely although already, in fact, a quick study by the British staffs had revealed the feasibility of attacking with six divisions in half the time originally imagined possible. On the morning of the 28th Montgomery gave Dempsey firm directions to launch what now became known as Operation 'Bluecoat', setting the 30th as the day for execution, committing four infantry divisions (one of them the left flank formation of US First Army) and three armoured divisions. They were to 'step on the gas for Vire'.

On July 28th, 5th US Division and the British 15th and 50th Divisions lay quietly watchful in defensive positions covering the zone selected for 'Bluecoat'. The remainder of the intended assault force – 43rd Infantry Division, 7th, 11th and Guards Armoured Divisions – were spread the length and breadth of Second Army's sector, some 76,800 men and 13,500 vehicles which had yet to be moved secretly, and partly by night, distances ranging between twenty-five and thirty miles. The security of their journey, made possible because the German Air Force had been virtually swept from the daytime skies of Normandy, took second place to swiftness of departure. Everything thus depended upon the prowess of small groups of staff officers at army, corps, division and brigade HQs to react with orders that kept pace with the current situation, the ability of the soldiers to apply correctly those orders – and the weather. Should rain fall and turn lanes into rutted tracks, or if there were fog, the most carefully prepared schedules might be reduced to chaos.

3 All in Movement

'I suppose,' said Stuart Pocock, as he completed a brief examination of Arthur Sykes's Movement Order, 'it will be a luxury when we're given more than a few hours grace for planning. This is as sharp as ever I want it, but well done Arthur. You did well to fix it so quickly. Let's hope it works!' He signed the order and turned again to study the map of the area for which the division was headed. The time was a little past 2000 hours, and the first serials of the division would not move off until 2330 hours. By then, he mused, there should be moonlight with good visibility – always provided the clouds stayed away, that mist did not form or the smoke from burning buildings did not intrude. He gave a passing thought to the hundred and one other units that would be funnelling westward to pour through the road bottlenecks near Caumont. Let just one lose its way or others, unconnected with this operation, infiltrate the area, then all would be thrown into a turmoil of snorting vehicles choking the narrow lanes. Eleventh Armoured was by no means the first formation scheduled to move. Hence the leading formations had been given even less time to prepare and, therefore, more scope for error. Down the Corps' main axis would travel the hundreds of tanks, carriers, guns and lorries of 6th Guards Tank Brigade, followed by 8th AGRA, and only after them 11th Armoured. It was too much to hope, despite careful route signing by the Corps Traffic Control Organization and the Military Police, that some units would not become inadvertently diverted or held up, and

22

that others from **XXX** Corps nearby would not crowd in from the left. There would be 'free runners', too, those like the advance parties of each formation and unit moving ahead to stake out claims for main bodies in their deployment areas and reconnoitre the battle front before formulating their plans. Distraction by enemy bombing, a broken bridge, a traffic accident: any of these could block a road and immediately reduce the tidy Movement Plan to a nightmare of hectic improvisation – and 11th Armoured Division, at the tail, would suffer worst of all.

Pocock had acquired a mental habit of matching the yardstick of theoretical Staff College exercises to the reality of war as a check against planning omissions and a measure of performance. He recalled the academic tendency to give instruction as though each stage of an operation took place as an entity, separated neatly in time from the next. In practice – and never more so than at this moment – each phase ran concurrently with another.

He rechecked the sequence of his staff's actions to ensure all was covered. Earlier the GOC had told him the contents of the Corps Commander's plan, but emphasizing that written confirmation, a formal Operation Order, was unlikely to appear before dawn. Nevertheless the GOC had hatched an outline plan for the division and passed it verbally to the brigade commanders, who in turn were transmitting their versions to armoured regiment and infantry battalion commanders. Within the hour Ferriers, Simcox and all the other unit commanders, briefed in outline, would be driving in cars and jeeps towards Caumont. The Gunners, meantime, always a law unto themselves, shaped plans they intended to superimpose upon all the others.

The CCRA, most senior Gunner in charge of 'Bluecoat' bombardment, was intent upon locating several score new battery positions within bombardment range of any target facing each respective divisional area. He had also to take account of the need to switch concentrated fire within the Corps area – to achieve what was known as a 'Victor' Target. But as yet he and his staff could only guess at the details of each brigade and unit plans within the guide-lines of the Corps Commander's scheme. Piously they might persuade and pray that local commanders would tailor their schemes to the orthodox, yet flexible, Gunner 'ideal' solution. Sanctimoniously they stood poised to step in and veto anything which might mitigate the guns' effectiveness. With good reason the Gunners rated themselves the crucial battle-winning factor, more powerful even than tankmen because they aimed to terrorize the enemy before a single tank or soldier advanced. They were aware, too, that a vast programme of aerial bombardment by heavy and medium bombers would strike targets at the extremity of field artillery range, thus leaving the crust of enemy front-line resistance unharmed and unshaken except for pummelling by the guns. But even Gunners have their masters and at Caumont it would be the logisticians who, in their endeavours to shift huge quantities of ammunition to the battery positions within the same time span as a vast redeployment of vehicles, could only deliver limited quantities to supplement the relatively small stocks already there. Thus the artillery programme might be restricted by a shell shortage rather than the number of guns. It all depended upon the success of the Movement Plan.

Next day, the 29th, the lower echelons of tank, infantry and artillery commanders would combine to reconnoitre the assault area, would share joint orders and then pass them to the lowest levels of fighting men – for action. Everything would be compressed by a miserly shortage of time. On the 28th only two corps leaders – the Commander himself and his CCRA – had actually viewed the selected battleground from the somewhat insecure front seats of two tiny unarmed Auster Air OPs, flying low, back and forth, across the tree-tops of dense *bocage*. Of the enemy they had seen nothing, but they were very impressed by the formidably thick hedges and banks surrounding the tiny fields. Yet the bare bones of the Orders that were being issued from HQ VIII Corps barely hinted at these problems. Tension, like the operation, was phased and at first centred in attention upon the extremely short notice allowed for the deployment, allied with individuals' cynical speculation as to whether everybody could actually arrive in time for the attack by 0700 hours on the 30th.

Imponderables such as these were concealed from the likes of Sergeant Grant in 1st Pentland Yeomanry. Sharing a bottle of beer with the squadron fitter sergeant, who had just completed fine adjustments to the five carburettors on his Sherman tank's multi-bank Chrysler engine, he stood up as young Andrew Partridge, his troop officer, approached. With studied casualness Partridge announced, 'We're off in a couple of hours. Tell the chaps to eat and be ready to move by 2300 – though I doubt if we'll start until a bit after that.'

'Any idea what's on?' Grant had asked.

'Not really. The whole Div's on the move, I gather. CO's gone off to an O Group at Brigade. Place is buzzing. The Adj's going round in circles. I don't reckon we'll get much kip tonight. Tell the boys to take all they can after they've eaten.'

Partridge strolled across to his own tank to speak to his crew, to make arrangements with them for his own meal and then fold his maps to give the necessary cover.

Grant's head poked through the bivouac flap where Armstrong was being initiated into the mysteries of Brag – his crew's standard procedure for relieving boredom and redistributing wealth after pay day. They took the news phlegmatically, repeated Grant's own question and obtained the same response. There was plenty of time. They reckoned to cook a hot meal and pack their equipment in a mere thirty minutes: with the meal excluded, it could be done in less than a tenth of that time. There had been an embarrassing episode near Gavrus when they left their kit behind – the sudden arrival of a German Panther tank had allowed little alternative. From that moment, high in the evolution of their tactical doctrine, appeared a resolve never to be caught without a brew of tea and the means to make one. They had given considerable thought to that problem because it was permanent: the matter of tank versus tank action was only momentary and occasional.

Noise level in the regimental harbour area rose, as it did throughout the entire divisional area and, indeed, most of the British Sector – the sound of dropped hatches, flapping bivouacs, hissing cookers. Canvas bundles and camouflage nets, lashed to turret sides and engine decks, softened the outline features of angular armoured walls. Crews became grouped in talk, commanders gathered to hear orders, check the allocation of radio frequencies and the reception arrangements at their destination. A petrol truck lurched by, its driver and his assistant offering fuel for last-minute topping up. In gathering dusk the squadron commanders received details of routes and timings from the Adjutant, then called together their troop officers, sergeant-majors and signal sergeants to transmit the information that would shape their movements that night. As an interlude four RAF Typhoon fighters, approaching to land at the nearby air-strip, were mistaken by Bofors gunners for something menacing and greeted in the gathering gloom with a roar of gunfire, joined by everybody else, so it seemed, who had a machine-gun handy. Men cursed and hugged the ground. Typhoons, fluttering like frightened fledgelings above the tree-tops, dropped their wheels in an attempt to look inoffensive. The racket ceased as suddenly as it had begun.

'After all that, Order of March is the Recce Troop, ourselves, RHQ, then "B" and "C", then the echelons,' announced Philip Snow to his leaders. 'Form up at the entrance to the orchard. I'll lead, then 1, 2, 3, 4, the fitters and ARV. We pick up the Corps route at the main road, two miles up the lane - but they've painted out the Corps sign to help maintain secrecy, so just look for an arrow and do as the Police say. Spacing and speeds as usual for night time, convoy lights only - but don't expect the pace to stay constant. A lot's going to be moving around tonight so for God's sake tell your drivers to keep their proper distance from the one in front - and pull off the road at halts. Anybody who breaks down will just be shoved off and catch up later.'

Two hours later Grant's driver drew in behind Partridge's tank in the middle of the field and switched off. It was a warm evening with a humming in the air, not just from the thousand motors that announced the beginning of the nightly, beach-head traffic shuffle, but from insects among the trees and hedges. This had been the inescapable background noise of their lives for weeks on end, lives encompassed by a turret's roof and the roar of machinery. Now occurred the precious interval between dusk and darkness when detectable, accentuated tranquillity transcended the quiet delight that, in peaceful days, was reserved for sunset. At this moment the war stood still.

The drone of the first enemy bomber, the glare from a searching flare, the rising arcs of tracer and blare from a hundred guns, firing broadcast into the night, broke the spell. Once more they were alerted by the eternal eager background to a Normandy beach-head night; the harbinger of fear which, nevertheless, brought scant confusion to a disciplined army; the disturber of sleep among a military population whose longing for rest was rarely satisfied and whose weariness frequently submerged the pangs of apprehension and fear.

'OK - mount and start up,' came a call from the dark. Crews clambered aboard, drivers and co-drivers wriggled through hatches into the warm hull's interior, signallers dropped into the turret to tend a radio set that, under wireless silence, they were forbidden to use. Gunners took their seats below the commander's feet, or lay on the engine deck, but none squatted atop the turret for fear of risking laceration – even decapitation – by the cat's-cradle of low-slung signal cable which criss-crossed the lanes in random profusion. Grant still bore the scar of his first encounter with a cable – an accident which had dragged him like a cork out of his hatchway. Head tucked low he adapted the turret flap as a wire-cutter.

Starters whirred and engines spluttered into life, the incandescent flicker of exhausts throwing tanks into momentary silhouette, the pin-point convoy tail-lights illuminating white-painted air deflectors delineating the column of waiting vehicles. Ahead the rising crackle from Recce Troop's revving Stuart light tanks told Grant that the regiment was moving on time. Headsets slung round his neck, he heard the Squadron Commander's engine roar. He picked up his microphone, touched the rubber mouthpiece to his upper lip, pressed the pressel switch and said 'OK, Topper, stand by'.

Below, in the driving compartment, Brown had watched the last of five red dashboard lights extinguish, telling him all five engine banks were at working temperature. He depressed the heavy clutch pedal, thrust the gear lever into 'First', and waited for Partridge's tank to lumber ahead until the convoy light seemed twenty yards off. Then down with throttle, out with the clutch as a thousand times before and they, too, were rolling, answering smoothly to touches of right, then left steering sticks. In the turret McAteer listened moodily to hiss and crackle in his headphones, hearing faint voices on adjoining frequencies that were no concern of his, ordered to listen but not to talk. The turret interior glowed from the red light of the 19 Set Power Amplifier as it hummed in its box. He dimmed the festoon lights, but in their subdued glimmer could still detect Grant's legs dangling the other side of the gun, could see the glint of brass rounds of 75mm ammunition. There was a time when the sight had enthralled him with its potential of romantic power. Now it scared him. His memories of that scene, only a week ago, when the enemy shot penetrated and threw all into sparks and smoke, shattering his illusions, introduced a distress he could hardly explain. The once-secure turret's interior had turned into a threatening place of prevalent danger once its old illusory invulnerability had been demolished. Alone of this crew, the new man, Armstrong, was divorced from their fears of reality, for in bivouac chatter they had kept their thoughts to themselves.

From orchard through lane to the junction with the main road the pace steadily accelerated until, in fourth gear, they were moving in excess of ten miles per hour, tracks throbbing in harmony as they rumbled westward. As yet they were tailing 8th AGRA and, so far, the Military Police had cleared the route of interlopers. From gloomy cottage doorways the Norman folk watched them pass; sensing, as perhaps everybody did, that something enormous was in train; knowing, from the latest bulletins, that the German front was cracking. Dust infiltrated everywhere, became mixed with petrol fumes and choked the atmosphere. The flicker of exhausts, random sparks from tracks on stones and shrouded police lights lit the way, the uneven growl and roar of engines filled the night with threatening sound. And overhead the bombers throbbed and searched.

The first halt came without warning, drivers hauling hard on steering levers to apply the brakes, as, suddenly, from the darkness in front, a convoy light loomed up as if to charge them. Inadvertently brought close nose to tail they waited at idling revs. 'Here we go again,' said Grant to Brown, but for only a couple of hundred yards, and with diminishing progress as time went by, each jerk forward a bit shorter, each waiting spell a little longer. Benstead felt cold. 'Let's come in please, sarge?' he asked and Grant shifted stiffly to allow the gunner to squeeze down into his turret seat.

Looming through a gap in the hedgerow he saw another tank – it looked like a Cromwell and therefore was not one of theirs.

'Who the Hell are you?' he shouted at its commander.

' "B" Squadron, 5th Tanks,' came the reply.

'What the Hell's 7th Armoured doing up here? I heard you should be miles away on another road. Sure you're not lost again?'

'Come off it. We just followed the one in front, then your shower got in the way. We can't be wrong. Must be you bloody amateurs.'

'Arrogant tanky,' groused Grant, emphasizing the acrimony he

felt for the Desert Rats of 7th Armoured whose veteran prowess
was much questioned by brash enthusiasts in 11th Armoured.
Notwithstanding their differences, the two formations were now
almost inextricably intertwined, compelled to make the best of
each other's company in an enormous traffic jam far beyond
solving at the stroke of a staff officer's pen.

Repartee such as resounded between individual sergeant tank
commanders spread to angry argument near the head of the
column where leaders of higher rank met in altercation. News of
the convergence by two divisions onto one road gradually
reached the ears of the Traffic Control Organization. Agitated
telephone calls passed heatedly between regulating posts. Staff
and military police groped amid the growing jam in suffocating
dust to filter machines from its centre and head them outwards
towards the empty routes they were intended to take. The drivers
of vehicles from units which had no right on the road, and which
were found intermingled with the particles of 7th and 11th
Armoured Divisions, became fair game for everybody's rage as
tempers frayed. Turret crewmen, hearing an officers' rumpus,
laughed and tried to sleep. Drivers, fed up with stopping and
starting, resigned themselves to fatigue, bitterly complaining that
their work was never done.

Time was passing and soon it would be daylight when this
mass of tanks, guns and lorries which, by dawn, ought to have
faded from view under camouflage in their battle assembly areas,
would be stranded and exposed to view in a nose-to-tail sprawl
– displayed to any passing enemy reconnaissance aircraft as a
blatant advertisement of the direction and magnitude of the
redistribution of strength taking place. On airfields in England
and in Normandy fighter pilots stood by to take off and give
cover as soon as it was light. At critical points along the route
anti-aircraft gunners set up their pieces, ready to fend off the
enemy should he decide to bomb so vulnerable a target. Grant,
freshly experienced, but well educated in the technique of
war, apprehensively recognizing the approaching crisis with a
perception equal to that of his officers, called for the Bren
machine-gun from below and went on 'following the one in
front' like a sheep into the pen.

Bit by bit order was restored as vehicles in scattered knots disentangled and made full throttle for Caumont, their commanders reading the Corps traffic signs and searching for the Release Point where guides stood anxiously to lead them into the next harbour area. By first light, however, much of 11th Armoured Division, as well as several more units, had not reached their destination. Tanks still blocked the road to troop carriers, self-propelled and towed guns. The ammunition dumping programme was falling into arrears. With common complaint everybody suffered choking dust which billowed from beneath passing wheels and tracks that ground the frail road surfaces into powder. And to dismount at the halts had its hazards, too, for they were entering a countryside heavily littered by threatening and familiar notices. 'Beware of Mines', 'Verges cleared to 10 feet' – fair warning of devices which might or might not be present but which, either way, must never be ignored.

Not until mid-day did Grant see the Release Point sign and the red-capped MP, his face and clothing the colour of stone from the dust, waving them by. For the first time in his life he recognized something reassuring about the Police. In the battle zone they were far less menacing than in peace-time barracks; they had an almost helpful air – and frequently there they were, standing at some shelled crossroads he would never loiter by. At last the squadron shook free the shackles of unwanted neighbours and made haste for the gateway to their next orchard harbour. High above were stencilled the contrails of wheeling Spitfires; at lower altitudes he saw still more orbiting. Grant, his eyes peeled for the skimming Messerschmitt that might suddenly swoop and spray them with cannon fire, was happily kept in safety from the Luftwaffe. More than twelve hours after starting and six hours late, they jogged alongside a hedge, switched off engine, flung off nets and bivouac, checked machinery for leaks, pulled out the cooker and began to prepare a meal. The smell of baked mud, hot oil and metal tainted the whiff of fresh grass. Petrol trucks bumped and whined in four-wheel drive from tank to tank, dumping jerricans of fumey 80 octane petrol plus lubricant for those machines that wanted it – truck drivers exchanging familiar jests with friends and comparing crude notes on the night's experience. A noise level which had risen to its crescendo began slowly to subside into a false calm, broken throughout the day by stragglers wending their way home, and by the comings and goings of planners and visitors.

4 The Sniper

Snug in his lair the sniper searched for prey. Private First Class Al Cherry was in his natural habitat in that, as a compulsive hunter, he was armed with a rifle with telescopic sight and was intent upon killing the game that was in season - at this particular moment, any German who chanced along. Not that Cherry had been a professional predator who spent all his time in the wilderness shooting animals. He was, in fact, the owner of a hardware store in Hancock, USA - a business which he ran before the war at a small profit that was just large enough to support himself and his mother. It was only at weekends, however, after he had locked up the store, that he found contentment, for then he took off in the Ford buckboard, heading for the mountains armed with an old Springfield rifle, to shoot whatever was hardest to stalk.

Cherry was fastidious about the nature of his quarry and abhorred killing for killing's sake. He did not even have the urge to shoot for the pot. To him the hunter's art was pre-eminent. Nobody ever asked why it was that he invariably pressed the trigger to administer a fatal shot. He could not have answered if they had. To him it was the pursuit alone that was justifiable along with its essential components - preparing the weapon, travelling to the hunting ground, finding a hide, seeking or waiting for the prey, moving into a good firing position unobserved, judging range and drift, drawing a bead and pressing the trigger to slay with the first shot. With mission defined and the

33

weapon provided for legitimate hunting, Al Cherry, one of the most law-abiding of Hancock's citizens, became a deadly killer governed by a ritual.

When they drafted Cherry in 1942 the United States Army was shrewd in allocating him to the trade that best suited his prowess – an unusual event, as many an embittered draftee might have been quick to exclaim. They made him a sniper and armed him, moreover, with a bolt-action Springfield .30 calibre rifle of 1903 pattern – the sort he knew best. It almost made the Army feel like a home from home. Taking this weapon as his most cherished possession, and provided with ample opportunity to practise with unlimited ammunition supplied by Uncle Sam's tax-payers, he asked for nothing better of life. Really, in the eighteen months' service that preceded his dispatch to Europe, the only ripples that disturbed a convivial routine came from an attempt to transfer him to the quartermaster's department as a storekeeper (firmly resisted along with suggestions that he might take promotion) and the exchange of the old Springfield for the new Garand M1 semi-automatic rifle. He objected as much to the Garand as to promotion, but the latter he could decline whereas he had to bid farewell to the Springfield since they were being withdrawn from service in his unit. He liked the Garand's 2.2 times telescopic sight, appreciating the balance of this rugged weapon, though he criticized, in concert with many small-arms connoisseurs, the eight-round clip with its minor disadvantages. By the time the 301st Infantry Regiment went into the line it could not be said that Cherry was as complete a master of the Garand as he had been of the Springfield; but it was rare that he shot badly.

The battlefield presented several new problems to Cherry. For a start he had not fully taken into account the quarry's power of retaliation – a power which, particularly when provoked, was quite terrifying. He learnt the lesson in his first engagement when he winged a German sentry but remained gawping at the scene of his deed. Enemy reaction had come hot and strong from artillery and mortar fire plastering the vicinity of his hide. He had been lucky to escape unscathed. It had been a shocking yet a profitable initial, practical experience. He had trembled for hours and could no longer hold the sights on a target. But it taught him extra caution. The second lesson had been more frightening still. On this occasion he had despised the Army's official training manual and omitted to provide a secondary hide for use if the first was discovered. He had allowed himself to be spotted by a German sniper and, for the next thirty minutes, for the first time in his life, found out what it was like to be hunted, dodging from cover to cover with bullets cracking close above his head, not once getting a glimpse of his tormentor. Only much later did he come to bless an opponent whose fieldcraft was superior to his but whose marksmanship was palpably inferior.

That was ten days ago. Since then he had matured. Moreover he could add two enemy dead to his original score. Now he snuggled hard by the east flank of the entire American Army, with Limeys somewhere to his left and, to his front, an enemy-held orchard, bounded by a lane, at a range of a hundred yards. It was the best-ever contrivance of hides he had achieved – and subtle too. Had he wished to occupy the dead tree on the extreme left – a traditional sniper's hide – he might easily have done so, but that was too obvious: a reference point for enemy counter-fire. He kept within the double-banked hedgerow that was typical of *bocage*, moving from place to place, taking cover from shot as well as from view, and thus provided himself with an almost inexhaustible variety of fire positions that would be difficult for an opponent to define. His orders were standard. Occupy the hide shortly before first light, carrying rations, water and ammunition for the day; keep observation on the enemy within his arc of vision; report what he saw; kill any German who exposed himself to view; return to base at last light; carry out ablutions, take a meal and sleep until he was called for the next day's stint. Just routine, but a routine which his commanders hoped would produce important information about the enemy as well as unnerving them.

The best hunting hour was at first light. Then, through binoculars, he might detect an unsuspecting target, some German standing-to in the misconception that he was invisible, un-silhouetted in the gloom. Then, too, there came the optimum spell, as the telescopic sight revealed more than the eye could detect and when its graticule just became definable in the ambient half-light. He calculated that a promising spot for a target to appear could be the gateway where a man might pass from one side to the other or stand to take advantage of the sweep of observation it gave. Another potentially attractive place was a battered water trough behind which, said some of the local 'sacks' in Able Company, lay a machine-gun nest. To these he gave special attention at dawn on July 29th.

Nor was he disappointed. Something moved in the gateway. Slowly and carefully he slid the M1 through its embrasure in the hedgerow, aligned the barrel with the gate and drew the butt to his shoulder, searching through the optic for the target his binoculars had revealed. But the telescope gathered less light than the binoculars and revealed only a grey haze in which the graticule was obscured. So patiently he waited for conditions to improve, employing the time, meanwhile, to quarter the sector through his binoculars for additional targets, memorizing, at the same time, the principal landmarks of this small sector of front.

A surprising amount of careless movement was taking place. Undoubtedly there was somebody lying close to the water trough, but also he was catching glimpses, through gaps torn by shell-bursts in the thick hedge as well as through the gateway, of activity deeper in the orchard. He spared time for a sweep of the ground in the British sector where it rose in a convex slope from the lane towards the tree-crowned crest. Once he thought he detected figures gliding along the hedgerow that led from the barn at the lane's side, making for the trees, but he could not be certain it was so. In any case, that was the Limeys' problem.

He checked the graticule's definition and found that against fainter types of background it was visible. In order of priority he re-examined those places where targets had appeared. There was nothing to be seen at the gateway while something which loomed among the apple trees was too hard to acquire, not worth the risk of a shot that would reveal his presence and, perhaps, his exact location. The first shot was the surprise shot, the one with most chance of killing. He might have to wait far longer for the next and by that time would have lost the half-light advantage. The man at the water trough was still in view, however, and quite plainly a machine-gunner. He could actually pick out the box of belted ammunition on one side. A swift re-scanning of points left and right and this enemy, he decided, should be the selected victim. The unknown German could as well have been a bear, a stag or a rat; simply, he had to be shot dead.

Again Cherry settled himself for a shot, hurrying the sequence of events just a little in case the target retired from view, but instinctively completing every item of the hunter's ritual, determined to kill and not to wound – above all not to miss. The butt was cuddled to his cheek, finger light upon the trigger, feeling the second pressure and squeezing harder until the rifle fired. The machine-gunner seemed hardly to move. Just a slight jump, but his head had dropped forward. Gently Cherry withdrew from the embrasure into the ditch's bottom and crawled fast to the left into the foxhole he had dug earlier that night.

Al Cherry had never heard of Field-Marshal Sir Archibald Wavell, but it is possible he would have disagreed with that distinguished soldier's definition of the infantryman as 'a suc-

cessful poacher, cat burglar, and gunman'. He would have opted
for a higher rating, that of 'athlete, stalker, and marksman'. The
point was that both definitions were apt in different circumstances - the difference between the common-or-garden man and
the expert. There was nothing common-or-garden about Cherry,
as he loftily tended to suggest to the other more mass-produced
members of his battalion. He was a specialist - and as such the
enraged Germans on the other side of the field now treated him.
For as a persistent and deadly killer-in-being he exercised an
influence far in excess of that of his fellow infantrymen who
remained docile until called upon for a co-ordinated effort in
attack or defence.

The problem now was to consolidate his pre-eminence. It was
encouraging that the enemy had refrained from counter-fire.
Presumably surprise had been complete and nobody had detected
his location by sound or rifle flash. So he could safely switch to
an alternative position and begin again.

Ten minutes later he was ready, observing the distant lane in
measurably better conditions of light, strongly conscious that the
Germans must be searching for him also. He had darkened his
hands and face and draped his head with a fine net for extra
camouflage. They had removed the dead man from the water
trough and there was nothing more to be seen there. But
something stirred by the gateway and he suspected some leaves
had been displaced close to the lane junction on his left. Of the
latter he could not be sure, so he concentrated upon the gate.
Yes! There was a head and now it was gone. He reckoned upon
it appearing again and took aim at its last point of entry. For
thirty seconds he tensed, sharply on the alert - and nothing
happened. So he relaxed, and the moment he did so there was the
head again. Taking a chance he drew a swift sight and fired. The
head popped back. He was uncertain if he had hit. Anyway the
head did not reappear.

Now it was their turn. A machine-gun combing the hedge to
his right, sweeping nearer. It might have been profitable to
search for that gun but he resisted the temptation. There was a
whole day ahead and it was wiser now to retire to the foxhole

and eat, to let the excitement subside and the enemy's vigilance slacken.

An hour later he was on watch again from his original position, trying to detect a target at the lane junction and seeing nothing; traversing right past trough and gate – and again finding nothing to shoot. It was mid-morning before anything further presented itself and again it was the man at the gate. This time he resisted the temptation to take a snap shot and waited in stealthy patience for a well-prepared engagement. Twice he watched the head appear, observe through binoculars, and withdraw. The third time he was ready and fired, splinters flying from the post adjacent to the head which immediately retracted.

He was not to know if he had killed for at once there was a vicious crack and turf kicked within six inches of his face.

'Christ, they've got me', he muttered, flopping into the ditch and wriggling sinuously as fast as he could go for the safety of the foxhole. Another bullet crashed through the branches and then the machine-gun chimed in again, showering him with splinters and leaves. Then something new joined in – mortars. The first bomb fell twenty yards left, the second a similar distance right – both good for range, it seemed. He awaited the third which landed a little left and short. There was a pause and he felt his heart pounding, hoping that was the lot, fearing it was the beginning. The approaching bomb sigh settled all doubt. Retribution was just beginning and, it seemed to him, was long to continue. The hedge and its compact banks shook but withstood the blasting. Once he feared the end as a deluge of earth fell on top of him from an impact within a yard of the hole, but he shook free and drew breath without showing himself above ground. The fear of burial was ever-present and the chance of rescue, in such isolation, remote.

When at last it was over he kept calm, though the instinct to run was very strong. He was shaken though not so badly as to conclude, first, that damage to the hedge might have destroyed his cover for retreat and, second, that an enemy who thought him incapacitated was best left to false conclusions. A careful investigation satisfied him that the cover was disturbed but basically intact. As to his second postulation, well, time alone would tell and he remembered an old soldier's advice, 'Never despise the enemy. He may seem stupid but he may also have been in the business longer than you'. Cherry warily added 'philosophy' to the attributes of a good infantryman – and this time waited until evening before again trying his luck, whiling away the time by momentary observations of the enemy.

5 *Bocage*

In the early morning light which had aided Cherry, Edward Simcox searched the somnolent panorama and sighed. At less than two hundred yards range reared the inevitable dense and high-banked hedge, obscuring the view and offering a practically impenetrable barrier except where it was breached by the lane on the left of the gate in the centre. The irregular, narrow gaps which had been torn by shells cleared the way hardly at all. Another hundred yards or so distant, he could indistinctly detect a parallel hedgerow as thick, if not thicker, than the rest, but farther than that it was impossible to read the country except by the glimpse of a farm's roof among trees, on the left, or the fringe of crestline tree-tops some four hundred yards from where he lay concealed. The only beasts in view were three dead cows, bellies distended with limbs as rigid as table legs, stinking in sickly putrefaction mid-field to his immediate front. Birds fluttered and sang, a light breeze ruffled the grass and leaves and wafted the smell of death their way. A mumble of guns stirred the air to east and south-west. Though the next hedgerow to his front was thinly populated by men of the 15th Scottish Division and the lane beyond by Germans, neither side made the slightest sound or movement. Only by night, as patrols stalked, when mines were laid, trenches improved and reliefs of the forward units completed did it alter the comatose siesta which furtively ruled by day. Here the combatants prosecuted a war of live and let live that was the pastime of battle-fatigued units. Simcox was their Nemesis.

He was perplexed by such inside information as he could glean from a map (scale 1:25000, overprinted with symbols that represented different, suspected enemy weapons, positions, field works and minefields); an annotated aerial photograph that needed an expert to interpret its meaning; and a report from Tim Parsons, whose platoon of 8th Gleneagles Highlanders occupied this length of hedgerow. Intelligence about the middle-distance enemy positions was quite profuse, but that of the foreground sparse. Apparently the farm on the left was strongly held and so, too, was the crest. But question-marks on the map littered the frontal enemy hedge and also hinted at mines. Parsons could add so very little to what was recorded on the map – indeed, in the main, the map's information reflected his own observations. Convinced, though he was, that the Germans had 'something in the hedge near the gate by the barn', he admitted neither seeing nor hearing it. Cautious examination through binoculars revealed nothing.

Simcox wriggled back down the bank to where his artillery Battery Commander, Major Brian Culpepper, and tank Squadron Commander, Philip Snow, squatted. They had spent the past two hours surveying the terrain and were confounded by the green walls of threatening blankness that lay ahead. The latest brisk exchange of fire in the American sector was uninformative.

'Can't say you boys have seen much that's of any help,' grumbled Simcox to Parsons. 'There's a ruddy great chunk of jungle down there that might just as well be Amazon for all we know what's inside it.'

'Sorry, sir,' replied Parsons, 'we've done our best to ferret about, but the mines made it difficult, and if you push your luck, down comes a stonking. I know – I was caught there myself on patrol a couple of night ago.' He paused at the memory of it. 'Their mortars have us taped. The company's lost half a dozen Jocks in the Three Cow Field as it is, let alone what the rest of the battalion's lost near Vertefeuille Farm.'

Simcox grunted. 'Do those stonks cover the whole of Three Cow Field?' he asked.

'Near as makes no difference – its centre comes down about midway across. They also put one on the Americans this morning close to our boundary. Bashing a sniper of theirs, I reckon.'

Simcox reflected upon the difficulties of arranging a quick attack at the best of times. Without a vestige of positive information it was tedious, to say the least. The previous afternoon his copy of the Warning Order had been followed within moments by the arrival of the Brigade Commander in person, and the Brigadier was clearly ill-briefed and under pressure from the Divisional Commander who seemed anxious to attack in some uncharted sector of the front at about forty-eight hours' notice. Never a man of lightning reactions Simcox resented haste, for he preferred to mull things over, to mature his ideas with time – and in detail.

'I can only give rough boundaries and an approximate objective at this stage,' the Brigadier had said. 'We're to lay on an attack early on the 30th. You'll have Culpepper's battery as usual and 'A' Squadron of Pentland Yeomanry. You can move independently, with your R Group, soon as you like, but make contact with 8th Gleneagles Highlanders before taking a look at the front.' There had followed a string of minor localities and timings. Then, 'I'll meet you in your Assembly Area at 1600 hours tomorrow to see if there's anything you want and co-ordinate the rest of the brigade's front.'

With a rare flash of inspiration Simcox had brought along Frank Davis and his patrol. While small, 'free-running' parties were permitted to go ahead of the main vehicle columns that soon would block every road from Bayeux to Caumont, he had seized the opportunity to have on hand a few trained men of his own for employment on any special task that might suggest itself. They had travelled at speed, spurred on by the knowledge that every moment counted. Lieutenant Buttonshaw, the Battalion Intelligence Officer, had read the map with shaded torch, urging on the Humber 'box saloon's' driver, narrowly averting collisions with ill-lit vehicles that groped their way by the flash of guns and a sultry moon, threading the way through gloomy lanes. Anxiously they were aware of a prevalent danger in unfamiliar country – that of navigating through the forward defended positions into enemy territory. The IO recalled how once, when approaching the front, he had become suspicious of a deathly silence and had halted to enquire his whereabouts from three men crawling towards him along the ditch. The rearguard of this patrol, in reply to his question 'Where's the front line?' had looked ponderously up and down the road and moved an extra yard before giving a considered opinion. 'At the moment, sir, you are!'

Simcox had sat in the back with Culpepper and Snow, debating their mutual problems. To Simcox, Culpepper was a well-known personality and predictable; his reactions to a prescribed situation calculable; his competence in controlling the fire of his guns in relation to rapidly changing situations beyond doubt; his natural dominance by strength of character in time of stress unresented. But Snow and his squadron were virtually strangers since, on those occasions the battalion had worked closely with the Armoured Brigade, it had been in co-operation with another of its regiments. Nevertheless, if Simcox shared the cynical infantryman's reservations concerning the average tank crew's lagging enthusiasm to risk their mounts in the forefront of the battle (though the last to doubt their courage in the light of what he had seen near Caen), Snow also harboured doubts about infantry, above all their capability to provide close escort for his tanks once enemy fire got hot. Again bravery was not in question. It was simply a matter of feasibility, of men's willingness to endure enemy fire in variable circumstances of stress. Yet somehow each must find a way to advance in strict accord with the other. Perhaps their paths would be smoothed by bomber and artillery power: in the final analysis, however, by sheer, organized guts and determination.

'There'll be bombers working over the rearward zone and the mediums and heavies from the AGRA will fill some of the gaps,' stated Culpepper. 'I'd like to suggest you use my battery to deal with known or likely anti-tank gun hides – or perhaps where some machine-gun is lying back – leaving Philip's tanks to sort out the forward edge of the battle.' They had settled for that while disputing the positioning of tanks in relation to the infantry. A familiar dispute began.

'I must have tanks ahead of my men to blast machine-guns

dug into the hedgerows,' claimed Simcox, hoping the new men would bend.

'I realize that, sir,' Snow had replied, 'but I'll do a better job from the flank or even from just behind your chaps as they advance, firing over their heads. You see,' he added quickly, seeing Simcox was about to object, 'with my neck stuck out too far my tanks are immediately vulnerable to bazookas in this close stuff while your chaps from behind me can give little help. In any case we can give better support if we stand slightly apart from the action. That way we get a wider field of view and fire, we're less involved and more discriminating in picking targets – and the fire directed at me will miss your men.'

They had argued and finally agreed to adopt Snow's methods, not so much because Simcox was satisfied with the arrangement but because he knew that, if he took the matter higher, Snow's Commanding Officer, Douglas Ferriers, would support his Squadron Commander and that, in the final court of appeal, the Divisional Commander (himself a tank man) would incline towards Snow's solution. They also agreed to detach the single troop of Firefly Shermans, with their powerful 17-pounder guns, from the forefront of the fight unless enemy tanks intervened. Not until they saw the ground, however, could any final decisions be made, and even then there might be problems with flanking formations which could compel them to alter their preconceptions. With 29th Armoured Brigade, the adjacent left-flank formation, problems were less likely because they had worked together before and respected each other's philosophy and methods. Fifth US Infantry Division on the immediate right, however, was quite likely to be another matter – a totally un-known quantity in every respect – foreign except for language, and even the latter, they feared, might raise difficulties when it came to a common military terminology. Simcox asked himself if the Americans might cause as much difficulty as the Germans.

Now, with the ground before them and clearly fraught with problems, the Germans a hidden threat, and the Americans only marks on a map (confirmed in presence by noises off where the sniper was active), Simcox felt frustrated and confused.

'I've got an RV with the Yank CO in about half an hour,' he

said to his supporters, 'so I can't really give you a firm plot 'til that's over. You never know how much he'll be able or even want to help - and the right flank certainly gives cause for concern. That orchard will have to be taken out if we're not to be taken in flank as we advance.'

'Yes, it's a bit too big for me to take on,' said Culpepper, 'and I can't yet be sure what help the AGRA will be in that direction. I take it the tanks can't do much? Or what about smoke, Philip?'

'With the prevailing wind as it is, it will blow right across us. Then what support I could give would be limited while the enemy'll be able to shift as he likes. Not for me! No smoke. It's still the dicey old two-edged weapon.'

'Well, anyway I'd prefer to put in my weight on the left, through Vertefeuille Farm,' announced Simcox, 'though I don't think we can leave the right unattended. While I'm away, work on the assumption I'll put a couple of companies down the left, where they'll get a certain amount of help from the Jocks, with a third on the right for good measure if the Yanks will join in. See you later at HQ, back in the barn.'

Simcox left to meet his American, the others to re-examine the ground to their front and approach routes on either flank, and still trying to pierce the enemy cover without being seen themselves.

In a cellar smelling strongly of cider apples and cheese, which the II 431st Infantry Battalion used as its headquarters, Obergefreiter Klaus Hauser kept watch, answering the telephone, moodily overhearing the officers' conversations and monitoring the changing face of the operations map that stood propped against the wall. Every eight hours the small-scale map of the entire Normandy front was altered to illustrate the changing situation on adjoining sectors, and always it was to highlight the advancing tide of American penetration down the western seaboard towards Avranches - infiltrating menacingly rearward of the line held by II 431st Battalion. Hauser cast a critical eye round the cellar, taking in walls that were covered by bed-sheets purloined from the house above, the maps, the office tables with papers and telephones on them, the duty officer's untidy camp bed in a corner; he sensed a brittle calmness in an atmosphere of insecurity.

The telephone buzzed and he lifted the receiver to hear his opposite number in Vertefeuille Farm reporting. He wrote on the message pad: 'Further to report of 0800 hours, another small enemy party observed opposite the Graben position, scanning our front.'

He passed the message to Leutnant Kurt Barentz who marked the information in crayon on the map showing the battalion's zone, annotating it with the time received.

'That's the second sighting of enemy observers this morning,' Barentz remarked to Major Jurgen Irkens, his battalion commander. 'There's been nothing like that for days.'

Irkens, a veteran from the Russian front where defensive fighting perennially absorbed the German Army, nodded. He had done everything possible with what little had been given him and could feel half-satisfied that, after a fortnight in occupation, this stretch of line was strong. Nevertheless he was despondent. Though the battalion was better provided for than some others, it was still only at half-strength and, of its three hundred and fifty men, many were of doubtful allegiance. If more than a hundred were German citizens in the purest sense of the word he would have been surprised. Some were Austrians, a few Czechs and several more were Poles. There were even a dozen Russians. Of his nine officers only six could be classified as reliable, but that was a reflection not only of the state of the regiment's training but of the entire German Army in the West. Of weapons there were sufficient and of ammunition enough for immediate needs, stored by weapon pits and in dumps near the mortars and guns. Transport, however, was at a premium – an incipient shortage made progressively worse by the depredations of the enemy air force which shot at everything that scurried by day, and much that crawled by night. In defence nothing could be expected from the Luftwaffe which they had long ago written-off as of no value in the land battle. The two anti-tank guns from the Regimental Anti-tank Company barely covered the battalion's area, and though 21st Panzer Division stood five miles off there was little prospect of its tanks being released for intervention in his area, especially since the tank component was already severely weakened. His role was therefore tied to a static defence that was symbolized by the very considerable number of mines his men had industriously laid, night after night, around their positions. A sparse, mobile, anti-tank force was provided by two armoured, self-propelled assault guns, attached from Division, and a single Jagdpanther, accidentally left over from Army reserve. These, the most powerful weapons in Irkens's command, lay hidden among trees behind the crest – uncalled upon, so far, to disclose their presence: with the pessimism of adverse experience, Irkens rated their chances of survival low once they were committed.

'Are the English looking hard at any particular place? And what of those Americans on the left?' he asked.

'The English,' replied Barentz, 'have appeared only on our right – but they could have been elsewhere. As for the Americans, they are quiet except for that damned sniper. We've been after him all morning. And that's another thing. We've not had that sort of trouble of late.'

'Well, if there's going to be an attack – and I quite expect there will – I wouldn't expect it to take place alongside the Americans. It takes too much fixing between Allies,' said Irkens, who recalled his personal difficulties in arranging close co-operation, quite recently, with Italians and Rumanians on the Russian front. 'It's much more likely to come further east or west. Anyway pass on the latest information to Regiment. Let them worry about it. Meantime let the mortars see what they can do if the sniper tries again.'

All this Klaus Hauser saw and heard. Better informed than most rankers in the battalion, he understood their vulnerability and feared for the future. A net seemed to be closing round them, and he was caught at the centre.

6 Traumerei

July was a month of acute crisis for the German Army in Normandy. From the east came news that, once more, Russian armies had broken through and were pouring into Poland, drawing ever closer to the Fatherland, rending the hearts of eastern Germans with fear for their families and homes. And from a village called St Foy de Montgomerie came a shattering report that Field-Marshal Rommel had been wounded – perhaps mortally – when his staff car had been attacked by British fighter aircraft. Into his place stepped Field-Marshal Günther von Kluge who, at the beginning of July, had replaced von Rundstedt as Commander-in-Chief. Fortuitously this healed the schism in the German command of the West just as Operation 'Goodwood' was being defeated on the 18th. However, the German defensive success was immediately tainted as news from the east got worse. Then, on the 20th, came an unprecedented upheaval – the unsuccessful attempt to assassinate Hitler, a plot in which both Rommel and Kluge were implicated. On the 25th the American break-through began and, with it, realization that military disruption, such as ran riot in Poland, was about to take place in Normandy. Von Kluge stated his point of view to Hitler on the 21st. 'I came here with the fixed determination of making effective your order to stand fast at any price. But now I have seen by experience that this price must be paid by the slow but sure annihilation of the force.' A week later, while the British and Americans made ready to strike southwards from Caumont,

Kluge's pessimism made a difficult situation more precarious. No longer was there confidence and no longer could interminable demands for help from fighting commanders be met from dwindling resources. As the frontage became distended by the bulging American penetration towards Avranches, the last remaining German hopes depended upon containment of apparent threats, to the exclusion of all else – succinctly expressed in a report by the Chief of Staff of Kluge's Army Group B. 'Army Group B will endeavour to prevent a breakthrough by *recklessly exposing* the fronts which are *not* being attacked.'

The front near Caumont, held by the attenuated 326th Division, was categorized as 'passive' and stood quiet in the aftermath of successful resistance to 5th US Division's initial attacks. Here was a division tasked to hold a frontage nine miles long, backed by the slenderest immediate reserve and with little else in support. Morale was stated as 'good', yet the men were told, when they entered the line:

'You are relieving an SS formation in a quiet sector. You will be opposed by troops of the 5th US Infantry Division who have suffered fairly heavy casualties. There is no armour against you. The enemy will drop, or fire over, leaflets. No one below the rank of major will pick them up. These leaflets invite you to desert and enjoy the amenities of British prisoner-of-war camps. Remember that if you do you will be taken to England and run the risk of death by V-1 [the pilotless bomb which at this time the Germans were directing against southern England]. After that you will be shipped to the United States or Canada for life-long labour. Or you may be exchanged for a British or American paratrooper (of which we have captured thousands), tried by court-martial and shot. In any case your families will suffer in consequence, exclusion from the German *Volksgemeinschaft* being the least of their resulting troubles.'

Threats such as these made slight impression upon hardened soldiers and only served further to confuse those whose first acquaintance with war this was. The American attacks, because they were supported by a deluge of shell fire and air attacks, had been chilling experiences, but, because 326th Division had stuck to its task, the propaganda line had held good. Nevertheless, several of the men queried the wisdom of further resistance. Would they be engulfed by the next American attack or escape because they happened to be out of the line in reserve or in course of transfer to another front? It was a toss-up which, for those going on duty at the front on the evening of the 29th, seemed likely to have spun against them. Their orders contained a trenchant note of warning. 'For tonight a special degree of watch is ordered. From statements of prisoners the enemy will attack our positions tomorrow morning, 30th July, at 0400.'

A platoon of Irkens's battalion tramping out of the line that evening remarked upon the increased enemy activity. That day a Scottish patrol, which had been intercepted, gave information of a big build-up, and the appearance at random moments of enemy observers keenly scanning their front all raised the tension. Moreover, was there not an increase in air activity and a faint rumble of tank movement in the distance to the north? The fears of impending danger which had filled Obergefreiter Hauser with foreboding now attacked his resolve. It was the futility of their condition which disturbed his composure. A letter that morning from his parents, who were under persistent aerial bombardment in the Ruhr, announced that his home had been reduced to ruins and that food was becoming scarcer. The letter had temporarily distracted attention from his own plight but, with evening, the fears of morning returned with redoubled force. From then on he worked automatically rather than intellectually, answering each telephone buzz in trepidity, dreading some fresh report of impending peril – news perhaps of an enemy force actually forming up to strike them. Voices on the telephone and from background conversations in the cellar became hollow, ethereally detached from the world of anxiety in which he drifted. When his relief arrived at 2000 hours he was almost exhausted. The sausage, black bread and ersatz coffee that waited for him in the farm-kitchen above he could not face. He pondered on how to avoid waves of suffocating threats; anxious to escape lest something indefinable should happen; only checked in his longing for evasion by a fellow-feeling for the others in the battalion who, he figured, might depend upon him and whose comradeship he valued. Barentz was loudly jesting with Irkens. Hauser despised and hated them for their light-heartedness. His officers' display of confidence might brace the others in the headquarters but, to him, it was a provocation which undermined his respect for those in authority. Hauser's lively imagination was overcoming the ingrained sense of discipline which had been implanted in him since childhood by parents who believed passionately in patriotic zeal. Had not his father fought throughout the First World War and regaled him with tales of heroism in the service of the Fatherland? Never had the cause seemed lost, or so he had been taught. But now some primitive insight seemed to credit the enemy with invincibility; it was contrary to the call of duty because it demanded he should survive. The struggle with his conscience further distracted him from work so that, gradually, he became morose, isolated in mind from those about him.

Deep, intellectual reasoning had always been at a premium in the life of Obergefreiter Otto Thoma, who commanded the six 81mm mortars dug in just under cover of the crest line. From here the most mobile of the German battalion's high-angle weapons kept up their spasmodic harrying of the enemy. Through the field telephone, from a hide dug close to the crest, Unteroffizier Hugo Dettinger directed their operations. He was near enough so that, in emergencies, it was sometimes possible to relay orders by shouting. Emergencies they preferred to avoid. That meant trouble and trouble enough they had had in the last few weeks. The threat of enemy aircraft was omnipresent. Two days ago one of the pestilential rocket-firing aircraft had engaged them and, though the missiles had veered away and exploded harmlessly, the rending sound of their approach had been terrifying. The most prevalent cause of fear, however, was enemy counter-bombardment. Although they frequently changed location after firing, it was uncomfortably evident that the British and Americans were adept at locating each new location within a short while of their disclosing it. Having once opened fire the period in action had to be short. Thoma knew that the battalion's heavy 120mm mortars suffered too, but, he complained tetchily, they were called upon less to engage. Something about ammunition shortage, it was said. Thoma, however, suspected that the Heavy Weapon Company Commander had a 'down' on him. There had been that unfortunate incident during training when, accidentally, he had fired short, nearly wiping out the fire-control post and with it the Company Commander. It had not been his fault: the mortar baseplate had dug into soft ground during firing and greatly altered each bomb's trajectory.

The telephone buzzed and he heard Dettinger calling for action, reeling off the ranges and bearings that were to be transmitted to the mortars. He shouted at the men and they tumbled from their dug-outs – three to a tube, to elevate and traverse, within the narrow limits imposed by its fixed baseplate design and cross level, as well as handle the supply of $7\frac{1}{2}$-lb bombs which, if required, they could drop, tail first, into the muzzle at a rate of about ten per minute. Within thirty seconds all six mortar detachments had reported their readiness and Thoma had told Dettinger. The target was a sniper; the intention to lay bombs along a hedgeline the range of which was previously carefully registered. Three sighting bombs were to be fired and then three rounds more per mortar. If they maimed or merely discouraged the man who twice that morning had killed, the ammunition would be well spent.

The loaders stripped packing material from the bombs while layers rechecked their instruments. Then:

'Fire.'

A loader slid a bomb into the muzzle, ducking aside to avoid the blast, and reached for the next bomb. The bomb dropped to the bottom, its detonator struck the pin and propelled it skywards. In their turn two more mortars fired, followed by a pause while Dettinger waited to see them explode with rending 'crumps' before deciding if corrections were needed. He was satisfied. There was a good mean-point of impact along the length of the hedgerow he had been ordered to attack.

'Three rounds each. Continue,' he ordered down the telephone.

'Three rounds per mortar, fire,' shouted Thoma, and all six

mortars coughed out a bomb, which was momentarily visible and climbed at a steep angle to its maximum altitude before tipping over and plunging to the target below. Three times each mortar gave its ringing cough.

'Finished,' reported Thoma over the telephone.

'Stand by,' said Dettinger, making a careful though rapid survey of the target. area where it stood cloaked in drifting smoke. It had been a good shoot. There was no need, in his opinion, to repeat it and the sooner his men were back under cover the better. 'Stand down,' he went on. 'That was good shooting. Right on target.'

'Stand down,' roared Thoma. 'Take cover.'

In an instant muzzle covers were replaced, loose bombs tucked away under protection, nets replaced above the pits and the men were leaping into their dug-outs. Here, with ears strained for the enemy counter-bombardment, they waited, preferring, however, to risk remaining in the present location rather than decamp, lugging the mortars to the alternative position, and chance being caught in the open. There was nobody among the mortar platoon of Hauser's sensitivity. They were rather unimaginative work-horses who traded punch for punch and did not count the cost except in terms of physical effort.

7 Counter-Bombardment

Concealed by long grass and dug-in deep in a pit near the centre of the field, Sergeant Reggie Banks listened attentively for extraneous noises, his ears tuned to separate the discharge of enemy mortars from the other battlefield sounds. Among the sounds he rejected were the ones made by that Yankee sniper, and the chattering response of the enemy machine-gun. He rejected, too, the bump of guns that lay outside the arc covered by the four microphones that were accurately aligned by survey in a row some thousand yards behind the front. From the Advanced Post, of which he was in command, he could, at the flick of a switch, turn them on when a mortar was heard within range, sending electric impulses by cable from the microphones' Short Base, as it was called, to the Command Post, still further in rear, where the acoustic disturbances would be visibly recorded on film - one display for each microphone.

Banks's fingers rested lightly on the control switch because, once he heard a mortar, his reactions had to be faster than the time it took the sound to pass him and reach the microphones.

There came another shot from the American sniper. 'That chap really is asking for it,' commented Banks to his companion. 'Jerry'll not put up with it much longer if he goes on like that.' They waited, then came the first mortar's cough. Banks switched on and reached for the telephone.

In the Command Post, more than a mile from Banks in a barn that stood close by the artillery battery positions it served, the

pen recorders whirred, reproducing tremors on the film until Banks switched off. Operator Number 3 intently read the film, chanting time intervals to the plotter (who was Number 5) while the booker (Number 4) wrote down the data with timed intervals. Meantime Banks was speaking on the telephone, sending in the standard Mortrep - the recording number, the bearing of the hostile sound, time of occurrence, the area attacked, type of enemy weapon, nature of bombardment, and number of bombs. The location was immediately recognized by the plotter. 'Same as Charlie Six,' he called, and at once the Signaller was sending this information by radio to the Assistant Counter Mortar Officer, who worked at the HQ of the CRA. Simultaneously the Command Post Number 1 was checking the data for accuracy and verifying it with Charlie Six on the map. Their task was complete but had to be repeated almost at once as Thoma dispatched his stream of bombs against Cherry.

Two hours before, Captain Douglas Anderson, the ACMO, would not have received a positive reaction to the report. The artillery's task for two or three days had merely been that of silent Counter-Bombardment - the logging of suspected locations and the drafting of a mosaic of enemy gun and mortar emplacements which assisted in an overall assessment of his deployment in this sector. Only rarely did the British guns hit back. Now there was a reversal of policy. The oncoming battle plan dictated that enemy artillery and mortars should be eliminated by active Counter-Bombardment at the earliest possible moment. The previous system of live and let live was to be abandoned. Every report was thus assured of creating a whirl of activity among artillery officers, their assistants and signallers. At once came permission to attack the offending mortars along with an allocation of specific guns and ammunition to each target, the calculation and transmission of data by telephone to regimental and battery command posts, instigating manual labour in the gun pits, the transfer of bearing and range setting to each gun, along with the preparation of ammunition and its subsequent resupply by lorry.

It took time to open fire – longer than it took Thoma's men to complete their task and retire to shelter. Yet within ten minutes of the decision to engage, the front reawoke. British guns pumped shells at the estimated position of the enemy mortars, raising flame, smoke and dust beyond the crest. They were right on target, searching the area of the German mortar position, filling the pits with earth and shattering one tube's sighting devices with a splinter neatly deflected from nearby trees. It went on like that for ten minutes. 'Good value for money,' remarked Banks, who had grown weary of passing information nobody seemed to want. 'Bloody hell,' complained the Jocks of 8th Gleneagles Highlanders as the shells whooped close overhead. 'We'll suffer for this.'

Silence returned. The British drew breath and awaited the Germans' response. American infantrymen indignantly asked each other, 'What Goddam bastard started all that?' and prayed for a return to the old monotony. But the Germans lay doggo. Dettinger appreciated that now was the time to shift his mortars to their alternative emplacements though warily in case the little high-wing monoplane, which skimmed the horizon beyond, should see them and call for yet another deluge of high explosive.

And Al Cherry, the cause of it all, settled down to brew coffee.

8 Negotiations

There was a pact between Edward Simcox and his driver that they did not speak unless Simcox spoke first. This was one of the silent days. Simcox was not only deep in thought but taking in the scene presented by the American sector in this, his first visit to that army since coming to France. His initially jaundiced opinion of this ally, formulated by random contacts with its members in the United Kingdom, was reinforced by first impressions. The atmosphere seemed more informal – to him regrettably so – than in the British Sector. There was little attempt to conceal the obvious signs of the military presence, a certain carelessness about the way vehicles were parked in the fields; hardly any precautions were taken to avoid detection from the air. Clearly these soldiers had never suffered as in the old days, when the German air force predominated back in 1940. The looser-fitting US combat dress gave a look of casualness to the soldiers in much the same manner as did their habit of address. There seemed scant attention to security. Take, for instance, the soldier of whom he asked the way to the HQ of 301st Battalion. 'Sure, bud,' he had replied fixing Simcox and his badges of rank with a look of friendly curiosity. 'Past the next intersection and you'll see a snowdrop. He marks it.' Both Simcox and his driver understood but only the driver grinned, surreptitiously, at his colonel's ill-disguised disgust.

Yet it had to be admitted by Simcox that there was something deadly purposeful about what he saw – about the execution of essential tasks, that was. Trucks moved fast and seemed to know where they were going. A battery of guns, half-concealed behind a coppice, looked clean and well protected by thick earthworks: the men were either asleep or at their posts. In a nearby orchard some tanks were being worked upon by men who seemed to merge with machinery. The 'snowdrop' treated Simcox with the same correct degree of suspicion and respect towards a stranger that he would have expected from one of his own military policemen. He was compelled to convince the man of his identity before being allowed to enter the farm: then he was saluted - and escorted. A sergeant led him into a farm house which looked somewhat the worse for wear, but whether from German or American depredations it was difficult to say. Sufficient to record, with disquiet of enemy intentions as well as respect for the Americans, that nobody was hanging about in the open: either they were in trenches or under cover.

What Simcox first saw of Lieutenant-Colonel Robin Callendar, commanding the 301st US Infantry Battalion, tended to make him concur with Irkens's opinion that co-operation with Allies was likely to be a dubious business. Here was a hard, practical man. Callendar, Simcox was later to learn, had been a Baltimore lawyer before the war, as well as a National Guardsman. He totally undermined the Englishman's preconceptions of the standard, boastful Yank, for, in an unsophisticated yet typically British manner, Simcox judged Americans by Hollywood standards. They met in a cellar which, minus sheets on the wall, was remarkably similar in its furnishings to that occupied by Irkens on the other side of the hill: lighting was provided by smoky kerosene lamps and the odour was precisely the same, give or take the characteristic aromas caused by their respective national diets and the tobacco they smoked. One battalion command post is much the same as another the world over. Moreover Simcox was given coffee to drink with a hospitality such as Irkens would have offered to a visitor - except that Callendar drank the real thing whereas Irkens made do with ersatz. Simcox accepted the beverage though he had secretly hoped for something alcoholic.

They got down to business with a minimum of introductions,

joined round the operations map by Major Bob Krantsky, the Battalion Executive Officer.

'They've told me what you're about, Colonel,' began Callendar. 'They say I'm to help if I can. I'll tell you straight, I don't like the look of that bit of real estate, not one little bit. And my tankers feel the same.'

There was silence – not one shred of an offer of practical assistance.

Simcox decided to project his ideas in their entirety at once and see what reaction that would bring. He presented to the Americans the same outline plan as he had left with Brian and Philip. 'The plain fact is,' he concluded, 'I don't much like what's on your flank, either, but even if I throw my full weight to the left, I still need assurance that the right is secure – that ground to your front is taken care of. Either the gunners can plaster it or they can smoke it – but better it should be occupied. Particularly that orchard. I've not the strength to do it. Have you?'

Deliberately he had adopted a down-to-earth approach like that employed by Callendar. Again there was silence – a silence Simcox left to take care of itself.

'Yeah,' said Callendar, shifting his chair.

'What d'y know,' softly mused his Exec – and waited.

Callendar put shrewd questions about the composition of Simcox's battalion and its experience – seeking in an instant to evaluate its potential and matching its quality to his own standards of military competence.

'See here, Colonel,' said Callendar at last. 'I'd like to help and seems you're talking straight. Your figures check with what I'm told. If I can be sure your guys will keep pace with me, I'm prepared to see what I can do to take out that orchard. But it's got to be simultaneous – no you waiting for me or me waiting for you. Most of all the latter. I'll add,' he said ruefully, 'we failed there once before on our own.'

Simcox was on the verge of retorting that the 1st East Hampshires waited for no man in battle, least of all for Americans, but he held back, superimposing his prewar training upon that of conditioned, soldierly belligerence. Another peace-time habit supervened. This man, it seemed, was adopting the bargaining position of a dyed-in-the-wool businessman.

'Look,' he responded. 'I always say a square deal's the one that satisfies both parties. I was a banker before becoming a soldier. It's as much in your interests to clear that orchard with my help as it's in mine to do it with yours. If I hadn't come along now you might have been told to try it again on your own tomorrow or the next day. I'm prepared to put a company - plus - along the edge of the orchard in a joint attack - with artillery and tank support shared. As security I'm even prepared to put that company under your command, if you feel that's necessary - though I'd rather it didn't 'cos I think it will be affected by what goes on elsewhere on my front.'

There was another pause.

'D'you drink rye, Colonel?' asked Callendar. ' 'Fraid we've got no scotch.'

'If you can spare it,' was Simcox's reply, recalling the meagre British ration, but Bob Krantsky was heading towards a full bottle concealed behind his Colonel's map display.

'OK, it's a deal, but there's no need for collateral and your men to come under my command,' said Callendar. 'The direction of the orchard hedge conforms to the axis of attack. That's plain enough. We can discuss later whether I go along the eastern edge or tackle it from the other side, working inwards your way. I'll be glad to put my Exec or somebody with a radio in your command post, though, so we can keep touch as things go on.'

The drink arrived in tin mugs - stiff tots by the look of it, thought Simcox - no shortages here. He suggested, 'I'll take you up on that. What's more we'll lay a telephone between your CP and my HQ so that we can talk without being overheard by Jerry. Cheers!'

At once they fell deep into detailed discussion, at a quicker pace than Simcox preferred, but crystallizing a half-formed plan before they were finished. As the spirit of rye and co-operation increased the use of first names replaced formality. After ten minutes they said their farewells. Simcox took Bob Krantsky with him, and found that officer rather more talkative when away from the presence of his Commanding Officer. From Krantsky

Simcox learnt about the outlook of the soldiers in 301st Infantry - itself a microcosm of the United States Army as a whole.

'They're mostly war-time enlistments - many of German extraction, incidentally - though a lot were drafted in with the National Guard before Pearl,' he explained. 'Precious few, I guess, know what the war's really about and fewer still are in it for ideological reasons. Most of 'em'll go when and where they're told - most of the time.'

'Not unlike mine,' interjected Simcox.

'Wouldn't know, but I guess you've got more regulars than we. One thing, though. We knock things down to get places. Somebody shoots at us, we shoot back - with interest and not just with hand guns. We give 'em it all - and it doesn't have to be Germans either who get it.'

'You mean yours shoot first and ask questions after?'

'Well, I wouldn't say passwords act awful strong as a deterrent.'

'I'll remember that and pass it on,' said Simcox thoughtfully. 'But tell me. If I sent a patrol near your rough vicinity, is there some sort of guarantee your lot will stay quiet while it's out - and desist from a shoot-up if something goes wrong?'

'Well, we can put a hold on small-arms fire and it might work - for a start. But if some of the boys thought they heard a kraut coming, well, they wouldn't care two bits about anybody else other than themselves. They'd just loose off. I mean, can you blame 'em? See here Colonel. I've been in a couple of fire fights. We've taken a beating here and I know what gives. It takes something to make a rifle or carbine man stand up and fire. They're waiting for somebody else to start, preferably with a weapon that gives off a good rasp of fire - the heavy weapons - the Brownings or the mortars. Better still the cannons. Now I can put an effective hold on the heavy weapons because they aren't so personally involved at the front. But you take a chance with the GIs - chances are they'll lie quiet, 'specially if they're told. But you just can't guarantee some brave bum won't choose any time to loose off on his own. If he does, the rest'll take it up from him. Get me?'

With that Simcox had to be content. Their destination was in sight, revealed by camouflaged jeeps drawn up under trees and outhouses near the barn they had appropriated as Battalion HQ. A plan was firm in his mind, clarified by pad jottings and lines, arrows and symbols drawn in chinagraph on the talc of his map. They gathered in the barn, the American was introduced – and a mug of tea appeared as of routine by hand of Simcox's servant. Simcox began the discussion by announcing that they could expect full and most generous co-operation from their American neighbours and that, therefore, the plan he had outlined a few hours previously more or less stood. 'Any second thoughts by any of you? Any new contributions?' he demanded.

Snow was ready. 'I've had a good look at the tank approaches and they are on, without coming long into enemy view, to within a field's length of our own front line. We can give solid support well forward once the attack begins, but I must ask that you keep within the scheme we discussed on the way down. That is, the tanks should stay in fairly close proximity to the infantry. Above all they must stay at least a hundred yards clear – clear of bazookas that is – on the left by the farm and on the right by the orchard.'

'All right, Philip, I understand your problem. Anything else?'

'Well, as soon as possible I'd like to know from Bob what the Americans are doing. What fire support will they give, how far left will they come and where will their tanks be? I'd hate one of theirs to pop through a hedge all unexpected and get shot by one of mine in thinking it was one of Jerry's.'

'Can't tell you yet – obviously,' replied Krantsky, 'but I don't reckon our tankers will go any further to their left than they have to. They're no more keen on deep *bocage* than you are.'

Culpepper was making signals to be heard. 'I wouldn't worry too much yet, Philip, about the American fire plan. I spoke with my CO a few minutes back and he says the CRA's fixing things with them. In fact, Colonel,' turning to Simcox, 'I gather we'll have an outline fire plan by 2000 – enough to build on, anyway.'

'It'll be comprehensive, I suppose?' asked Simcox, with a grin.

'But of course,' replied Culpepper who, like all artillerymen, believed in the virtues of science.

'Very well then,' said Simcox, 'I think we can break up for the time being. The division should be almost complete, but they've had traffic troubles on the way down I hear. I should be ready to hold my O Group here at 1700 hours. I imagine the Brigadier will let me have his final instructions at 1600. There's just one thing I'm not happy about. That is, what goes on in the area of that barn near the enemy front line? Bob, have you anything on it? Your left-hand platoon must have a sight of it?'

'None, sir. They mortar not far from there sometimes and we can't believe there's nothing there. But we've seen damn all.'

'No different to the Gleneagles. OK, we must have a look at it early tonight. Sturrock,' he called over his shoulder, 'ask Mr Davis if he'd be kind enough to step this way.' He turned to the others. 'I've already got an arrangement with the Gleneagles to put a patrol out in their area tonight and I'm going to take up the option. Philip, you needn't stay unless you want to, but Bob, I'd like you to remain behind since this could affect your chaps - and you too, Brian, for whatever pickings the gunners can get out of it.'

A movement in the entrance of the barn showed two figures silhouetted - one Davis, the other David Garston, Davis's Company Commander.

'Hullo, David,' said Simcox, surprised. 'How did you get here?'

Garston saluted and grinned. 'They said there was a traffic jam last night, but I slipped on ahead to see what was what, particularly since I rather gathered we might be in the lead.'

'Well, you might not - but glad to see you. Join the party.'

Snow stood up, saluted and left. Davis and his Company Commander gathered round and listened attentively as their CO gave out instructions.

9 Orders

They were all a little out of breath when they met again in the
barn for Simcox's O Group. 'Gentlemen,' he began, 'let me say
from the outset that this is among the hastiest operations ever
foisted upon this battalion – yes, even including exercises in
England.' Simcox always delighted in an excuse to show his
contempt for the authoritarian mien of conventional regular
officers. He detected subdued grins from the group who squatted
in the dim light of the barn. The old hands understood their
colonel and also recalled how this division used to train hard
against the clock – in days when the 'enemy' was less to be feared
than a dynamic divisional commander. It came home to Simcox,
with a jolt, that more than half the cast of his normal Order
Group was different. David Garston and John Codrington were,
in fact, sole survivors among the company commanders who had
crossed the Channel six weeks ago. There was a new mortar
platoon commander, too, in addition to such strangers as Snow
and Krantsky. It was almost a relief to see the well-tried
Culpepper sitting beside the original Adjutant, Dick Tranter.

'A word of warning! Jerry sometimes lobs shells into this
hamlet. If he does, turn right out of the door and hastily past the
dead horse. You'll find quite a deep ditch running close behind
the barn. Sorry about the horse, but he bought it only an hour
ago and we've not had time to remove him.' Nobody laughed.
'Now, the ground's been explained to you and you've an idea of
what's in store. Information of the enemy, while profuse about

his higher organization and optimistic that we are faced by a single, understrength division, is mighty short of what matters. You've got the overprinted maps, but we've nothing positive concerning his armour – only that it's pretty clear no Panzer Division's in range though there's every reason to expect some SPs to turn up. It's also pretty clear to me that we can expect him to base his defence of the left on Vertefeuille Farm; of the centre on the tall trees that cover the crest and on the right where the lane joins the orchard at the junction with the Americans.'

He paused, adding emphasis to each area by pointing to the large-scale map propped up before them.

'The front's covered by the usual sort of mortar DF. There's a rash of 'em that come down just this side of the lane. I think, too, we can expect the usual reception in the obvious FUPs – so we'll avoid them as much as possible. Finally the whole place is stiff with mines – theirs and ours with no guarantee the Sappers will lift even all of ours before daylight. Any questions so far?'

'I gather there's some sort of worry something might be holed up in the barn?' prompted Garston.

'Yes. As you know, David, Frank Davis will be sniffing around after dark and you'll all be told the result when he gets back. There could well be something there, if only by night. Any more? Sorry, but we must push on. There's so little time and I doubt even now if all your chaps will have the chance to view the ground before we start tomorrow.'

Simcox flicked a page of his notebook. 'Well, you'll have gathered 11th Armoured Div, as part of VIII Corps, is going to attack to the south of Caumont. Fifteenth Scottish are going in on our left and the American 5th Division is taking part on our right. Some of you have already met Major Bob Krantsky of their 301st Infantry. He's here to ensure liaison and generally make sure we don't get all snarled up. Bob, I gather we'll have your Colonel's plan quite soon but that he intends to attack a little apart from us, taking out the orchard from the west?'

'Sure, sir. That's what he said on the telephone a moment ago. I guess he'll start a little after you, though, in order to let the dust from your bombardment settle. But it'll only be a matter of minutes.'

'OK,' said Simcox. 'Now, on our own front we've adopted the new system of grouping, mixing the armour in heavier proportion to ourselves, and that's why 'A' Squadron of the Pentlands is with us along with the rest of the regiment's tanks coming on behind. The division has been told to protect the right flank of the British attack while our brigade has the task of securing the division's right - so we may have the more important and perhaps the most lucrative role. We've been given a lot of extra artillery, some Flails and some Crocs too.'

He turned another page, looked round his officers to gauge their mood and ponderously announced the battalion's role.

'1st East Hampshires will seize and hold the Vertefeuille crest.'

How often in the past had Simcox given out what was officially entitled The Intention? Yet only since their induction in real combat had its true meaning dawned upon him. He had come to notice in the heat of action how those who had closely understood the Intention had also maintained the struggle, while those who brushed it aside in their anxiety to hear his plan had fallen down on the job, failing to press through to the objective when the confusion of fighting had created a plethora of distractions. So he repeated the Intention and added, 'That above all, gentlemen - let there be no digressions in the interests of improvised flexibility.'

They laughed and the diligent underlined their notes while others drew heavier chinagraph marks upon the talc covering their maps.

'All right - Method,' went on Simcox, using the regulation term. 'We will advance two up, 'A' Company on the right, 'C' left with 'B' in reserve. Objectives, Phase I. Right, line of the lane from junction with the orchard to crest of the ridge. Left, Vertefeuille Farm with exploitation into the copse. Phase II. 'B' Company to pass through 'C' Company on the left to secure the Crest Copse, moving on my order. Start line, line of the hedge which is the existing FDL. 'A' Squadron of the Pentland Yeomanry will be under command and will allocate a troop each in support of 'A' and 'C' Company - the remainder of the squadron will give general support and, of great importance, will position itself to deal with any German armour coming into action across the ridge. OK, Philip?'

'Fine Colonel,' said the tank commander. 'I'll probably keep what's left to me fairly central – the Firefly troop in particular – and be ready to go with 'B' Company when you commit them.'

'I'll come to that later. In the meantime the fire support we may expect is pretty extensive. I'll just mention that fighter bombers will take on the enemy mortar and machine-gun positions as from first light and then over 700 heavy bombers and 850 mediums will be sharing out their wares between our Corps and XXX Corps – of which our division gets the direct help of 300 mediums which will bomb a box some 4,000 yards beyond the start line. They'll not start bombing, however, 'til two hours after H hour. On the other hand, you'll also be pleased to hear that they will use fragmentation bombs to avoid that ghastly cratering we saw near Caen. Brian Culpepper will now say what the gunners can do for us. Brian!'

The Colonel sat down, his place at the map taken by the Gunner, who clutched a formidable-looking table of Fire Support Tasks.

'This all looks very complicated, I know,' he began apologetically, 'but in fact the speed of events has led to an arbitrary sort of plan being superimposed by the CCRA – so arbitrary that we've got a smaller share than 29th Brigade on the left. They've – Corps that is – have gone for simplicity – counter-battery work from now onwards, linear barrages here – and here to be supplied by the Field Regiment and a concentration by a battery of mediums from 8th AGRA on Vertefeuille Farm.' He pointed to each target in turn, marked by lines and crosses on the map. 'Of course, in addition there are the Americans. *They* are going to put concentrations on the orchard timed to fit in with our movements as well as their own. Now, the timing of these concentrations is precise and cannot be interfered with during the initial assault – which is Phase I in the division's plan. After that, however, we can pick opportunity targets – those which seem most demanding of attention. Your Colonel and I have chosen places that look as if they might give trouble. I believe I'm right in saying, too, that you're keeping back your mortars for special tasks?'

'Yes – I'll deal with that now, Brian, if you've finished. OK. Freddy!' Simcox turned to Pascoe, the replacement mortar platoon commander. 'Your chance to make friends. I'll want one of your sections to put smoke on Vertefeuille Copse from H minus 5 to H plus 15 and thereafter maintain normal rates of fire on the same target up to H plus 40 or until success at the farm is reported. The remainder of your platoon is to maintain fire on the crest line where the lane crosses on the right there. Do that from H until H plus 40 and then await my orders. So much for fire support . . .'

He was cut short by the roar of a jeep followed by a flood of bad language from a voice he recognized as that of Sergeant Barstow, the Provost Sergeant. 'Catch hold of that bloody man and ask him if he wants to get us stonked to Hell. Tell him to bloody well slow down. There's a cloud of dust a mile high. Every Jerry in sight will have seen it . . .' and a lot more besides.

'As I was saying. So much for fire support . . .' but again he was interrupted and this time by the swish of a falling shell followed by its rasping crunch; then a second howling down in close succession. Dust and debris showered from the rafters and mixed with the smell of explosives that drifted through the doors. Irresolute officers ducked and looked at their commander. Some made retrograde motions and a newcomer hid behind a beam. But Simcox stood still and fixedly regarded his Adjutant who was pencilling deliberate and rather ostentatious squirls on his pad. From outside came another whistle, another crash and this time the cries of men in confusion and pain.

'I think we'd better break it up for a bit,' remarked Simcox. 'Don't rush. And don't forget it's right out of the door and just past the horse.'

The evacuation proceeded smoothly, led at a measured pace by Simcox in close company with his field officers, though it was noticed by Sergeant Barstow, from where he lay near the farm's midden, that the arrival of the next batch of German shells produced a distinct acceleration among the officers, certain individuals overtaking their Colonel who never for a moment increased his pace.

'I trust,' said Simcox to Culpepper as they crouched in the

ditch, 'that your colleagues will be fully engaged in a bit of counter-battery work? It's bad enough having one's O Group interrupted but I don't want that sort of thing tomorrow morning.'

'I'll check, Colonel, although I know Corps have sound-ranging bases laid out, so they should get onto that lot quite smartly.'

Almost in immediate response, it seemed, there came a distant 'bong' from the north and the whisper of a shell overhead. Culpepper and Simcox grinned at each other. This was service indeed – and in good measure, too, as a volley of 'bongs' sounded out and the air was rippled with the rustle of shells and their distant 'crumps' in the region where the locating devices said they had found the German guns. For five minutes it went on – a period of recuperation for those in the ditch to stand up and for work in the headquarters to begin once more. Felix Chandler trotted past, followed by a medical orderly, and joined a small group rummaging in the ruins of an outhouse that had been struck. Simcox walked over and saw a signaller stretched flat, pale and blood-stained, with Chandler beginning an examination.

'Bad, Doc?' asked the Colonel.

'Not too good. Mostly internal stuff. He's "out" at the moment. What bloody fool kicked up all the dust? That's the second time today.'

Simcox knew he could leave the Provost Sergeant to deal with that and, with approval, observed Barstow and the RSM already in heated conversation and pointing towards the jeep park under the trees.

'Let's get back to work,' he called.

On the Vertefeuille Crest a German Artillery OP Officer, Oberleutnant Klaus von Schilling, logged the time and location of the engagement along with the comment: 'Dust cloud engaged with ten rounds at previously suspected enemy location. Results unobserved. Enemy counter-battery fire drawn.' And back in his battery they, like the East Hampshires, were counting the cost – a gunner laid out by splinters from an enemy shell, a truck with its sides riddled and its tyres flat.

They sat more timidly in the barn, fearing another interruption
– which rather suited Simcox because it would hasten the O
Group by reducing the volume of questions that might follow.
Time was more pressing than ever before. He dealt swiftly with
the role of the four medium machine-guns that had been
attached from brigade, giving them the task of firing a steady
barrage of bullets first on the farm and then along the crest. For
the 6-pounder anti-tank guns there was only the job of driving
forward to the final objective, as soon as possible after it had
been reached by 'B' Company, there to consolidate the position
and await the tank counter-attack they felt sure must come –
even though it was claimed no enemy tanks were in the area.

'What disturbs me,' went on Simcox, 'is the mine business.
The place is stiff with 'em and the sappers are flat out trying to
open up wide-enough routes to the start line. They've been told
to open a corridor 600 yards wide, but they'll never make it in
time. The flails are to hand, but,' turning to Lieutenant Keith
Duncan, their officer, 'as you know I've no positive job for you
to begin with. So I'd like you to position yourself close to the
start line at H plus 10 and wait for things to happen.'

Next came timings – H hour fixed for 0700 hours – communication arrangements (wireless silence until H minus 3
hours), and administrative details of which the positioning of the
Battalion Aid Post along with evacuation of casualties took pride
of place. For this task the carrier platoon could be spared, for in
the *bocage* the fighting capability of the open-topped tracked
vehicles was severely impaired. Then came the moment for
questions, when Simcox hoped to be flattered by their scarcity
and brevity. They all, he knew, wanted to get away to make their
own preparations, to complete their personal reconnoitring and
give their own orders. He knew, too, that they expected him to
tour their locations before H hour and tidy up such loose ends
as had appeared in the latter stages of planning. But it was not
to be. John Codrington, the commander of 'C' Company, had his
hand raised, like a schoolboy asking to be excused. 'Yes, John?'

'I'm a bit fussed about the extent of the task you've given me,

sir. I know the gunners will take the farm apart and they hope
to snuff the German artillery before we get started. But that farm
is a lump of a place and I'm only seventy-five per cent up to
strength and I'm afraid we'll have our work cut out trying to
subdue it if the Hun makes a fight of it.'

'Don't forget the fighter bombers will have had a go, too, and
that 29th Brigade are working through on the left,' reminded
Simcox.

'Mm – but with respect to the RAF they aren't all that
accurate or as reliable as the gunners – take a bow, Brian. We
can't rely on them. But David relies on me to clear the way for
him and upon that depends the whole show. Can't we have 'A'
Company in a little closer, leaving only a guard on the right
flank? Can't I also have additional fire support – more mediums
if possible – to thicken up the initial bombardment and spread it
along the lane to the right?'

'We can't tinker around with the right flank,' stated Simcox.
'The Americans depend on us there. Brian, any hope of
something extra?'

'I can ask, but I shouldn't raise your hopes too high. There's
a slight ammunition shortage to begin with. I could have the
existing linear concentration shifted a bit to the right to take in
more of the lane. Would that help John?'

'Not really – sorry, but that's just robbing Peter to pay Paul.
What I really want is more men – at least another platoon so I
can take out the lane with it and put the entire company – all
three platoons – into the farm.'

'Would it help if I lent John one of mine for Phase I?' asked
Garston of Simcox.

'It might, but I want your full strength on the final objective.
No, not that, David.'

'How about that platoon of Jocks who are there now?' suggested Snow. 'Couldn't they come under John's wing and move
forward in conjunction?'

'And leave the start line unprotected?' interjected Simcox.

'Not if I fill it with my men,' said Garston.

They looked hard at Simcox whose chin was resting in his
hand.

'Sir, if I might suggest . . .' began Dick Tranter.

'Not just now, Dick,' cut in Simcox.

There was a long pause and then, 'All right, John, I see your point though I think you're exaggerating a bit. I'll have a word with the CO of the Gleneagles and let you know the outcome. But, David, you'll have somehow to arrange security without exposing your men to additional movement after H hour. I don't want them taking over the lane from the Gleneagles as they move out. Remember, your main job is to seize that crest at the right time. You must hold the front from a field or so back without getting in the way of all the DF that might come down. Let Dick Tranter know your plan later? OK? Any more?' There was none. 'Very well, gentlemen, that's all. You will receive any additional information that comes in during the night – including the result of Frank Davis's patrol. Good luck.'

It would be wrong to suppose that the dispersing group at this moment had anything but the haziest notion of what they might expect next day. Only Simcox, Culpepper and Snow had a comprehensive understanding of the scheme afoot, and, of these three, Culpepper was probably the best informed of all – as was common among gunners with their privileged insight, through superior communication channels, into high-level planning.

Codrington's reservations and the support he had received from the others had inspired doubts in Simcox. He was angrily conscious of deficiencies in his training and, of instant concern, his approach to this particular action. Perhaps his orders had been too informal. There had been far too many interjections. Or was that not permissible? The emphasis of his indoctrination as a battalion commander in a lorried infantry brigade, as part of an armoured division, had fallen upon quickly arranged attacks that were mounted to take advantage of fleeting situations. Practice in the preparation of deliberate attacks, such as now faced him, had been low in priority since they lay in the province of battalions in ordinary Infantry Divisions. He found himself wondering if his plan was wrongly directed against a well-prepared enemy – wrong, that is, for using insufficient men and not enough fire support at a selected spot and thus giving the enemy too much latitude. Simcox harboured misgivings about diluting his efforts and ruefully asked himself if the commitment to close co-operation with that American, Callendar, had not been mis-conceived. After all, there was no guarantee that the Americans would come up to scratch or, even if they did, that their efforts would unhinge the German position. Well, there was nothing much he could do to alter things in that direction. That was the devil of it! He simply must get the use of that Scottish platoon. Then he would just sweat it out - and give thought to an alternative, emergency plan if things went wrong.

10 Why Advance at All?

The squad were making last-minute preparations for the return to the front with the rest of Company Baker, to take their place alongside Company Able. Corporal Joe Carter, the leader, was wiping his mess tins clean prior to tucking them away among his other personal belongings in his haversack. Hoffman and Petersen were rolling the waterproof bivouacs that had sheltered them in the double ditch; they preferred working together. Novak sat cross-legged, once more oiling the breach and bolt of his M1 rifle - for the umpteenth time that day: he was a gun-enthusiast. Holmberg, good Pennsylvanian countryman that he was, dug deeply nearby, burying the remains of the day's waste, the beans left uneaten, the K packs that had been opened and left unconsumed. In a recess cut into the ditch on top of one of the little hexamine tablet fuelled stoves so obligingly discarded by the Germans, coffee boiled. Soon they would be drinking it fresh, and then it would be dark and they could be moving off. A hundred yards to the left Carter discerned the Englishmen of the squad he had talked to that day, men with simpler equipment but attitudes remarkably like his own to the war. They fought, it seemed, because there was a job to be done. They took an impersonal view of the enemy too: all, that is, except the SS who were feared and hated like vermin. Carter had it in mind to remain a regular soldier after the war and there were two regulars among those British - which was two more than in his own squad.

'Coffee,' announced Petersen in his thick accent. Petersen, like his friend Hoffman, was of German extraction, second generation and both hailing from Winchester in the Shenandoah Valley. They gathered round while he lifted the can from the flame and began pouring its contents in each man's mess tin. This was the best pot, the one to complete a day of rest in which they had fed, cleaned their arms, written letters and slept. There had not been a mail call, but at mid-day a hot meal had arrived in an insulated pot. That had tasted good. Then they had been told that they were to attack again over the old ground and against an enemy who had defeated them at the same place less than a week previously. That was not so good; neither was the news that the British would advance alongside them greeted with unanimous approval.

'What can they do that we can't?' asked Novak. 'Who are they, huh? Look how fast they've gone up their end and how much more our guys've done down here.'

'And look how fast we've gone just here,' derided Holmberg, the Dutchman. 'Hell, man, it's same for us all. If the kraut wants to fight, we fight an' we go no faster'n he let us.'

'Well, why the Hell should we help the Limeys?' demanded Novak. 'It's their war. They started it. What d' we get from it?'

'For me,' said Holmberg, 'a job after two years on the bum. OK, I was drafted like the rest of you, but I was glad. I live better this last two years.'

'Yeah but you gottan interest. You got people in Holland,' protested Novak.

'So what? I don't know them, they're just names,' came the reply, 'and how about Hoffman and Petersen here? They're Germans. How do they feel?'

Carter listened attentively. They had talked it over before in the days of training in Louisiana, on the transport coming over, then in Northern Ireland. But this was the first time since that they had experienced combat. The old dilemma - why do we fight for an indistinct cause? Why advance at all!

'You none of you know what you talk about. You talk crap,' rumbled Petersen, pouring the last dregs of coffee into his own tin. 'We Germans from Shenandoah Valley are drafted like

Novak from Baltimore and Holmberg from Gettysberg. We do as we're told. There's trouble if we don't. We want no trouble.'

'So you say. But what d'yer think now? How 'bout that kraut you got last week? What if he was your cousin?'

'Him or me,' replied Petersen simply. 'He was pointing at me. I just had the draw. I do not like it.'

'Who here likes to kill anyway?' asked Carter.

'You are right to ask,' put in Hoffman. 'It's not easy. I shoot at a hedge with the BAR. Who knows what I hit? I see that guy Fred kill and the big one beyond. It's a big effort to shoot that kraut even though I know it's him or Fred.'

There was a brief silence until Holmberg spoke again. 'It was sure easier after that. I felt bad over them two guys, too, but later when we got close I throwed the pineapple right among that bunch in the doorway. You sh'd heard 'em shout!'

'Funny thing that,' said Carter. 'Lieutenant Briggs was telling me 'bout a bunch of guys in a fight just after they landed. Seems they got among a load of krauts and went berserk. Nobody could stop 'em. They shot everything in sight including all the pigs and cattle in a farmhouse. I told it to a Limey today. He said he knew what I meant. Felt the same way himself after being mortared hours on end and when they came across some krauts just after.'

'Makes you see how the atrocity stories start, don't it?' said Petersen. 'My Pa told me how people thought every German was a murderer in the First War. He saw it all from the German side but nothing like that – but *they* were damned sure the British and the French were murderers too.'

'There's the Irish in Able Company who'd rather fight Limeys than Germans,' put in Novak.

'Aw, they fight anyone,' said Carter. 'R'member time we had to haul 'em out of that joint in Belfast? Those were Irish – their own people they were fighting then.'

'Well, tomorrow you fight Germans and you see the British fight,' said Petersen to Novak. 'Then you compare – if you got time. Me, I lie low and hope nobody notice.'

'I see no good in a Limey,' said Novak on principle, though he had never seriously analysed his views of an ally he had once heard complain about the Americans being overpaid.

They swallowed the last coffee grains and completed their packing. Lieutenant Briggs walked along the hedgerow. Carter saluted. 'Still sucking for promotion,' muttered Novak. 'Or maybe he makes a home in the Army?'

'Move in half an hour,' said the officer. 'We pick up a guide by the dead tree and he'll take us into the line. You're on the left. There'll be a British officer waiting to show us their location. I'll be there with you too. Just two more things. There's a post of ours just front of where you'll be. Tell your men. and we jump off just after seven in the morning. Don't tell them that yet, but have them ready. I'll tell you more about five tomorrow. We're in first of the 301st, but the British are going on ahead of us, so it'll be better than last time. They'll take the rap.'

'What happens if things blow on the left during the night?' asked Carter. 'Do we shoot back?'

'Gee, I'm glad you asked that. Well, the Exec says we're to hold our fire as the Brits have a patrol out. So hold your fire, but not so's the enemy knows. Who knows what the Limeys'll do if things get rough. We've no reason to trust them.'

'Any more than they us,' thought Carter – but kept his counsel and went to brief his men.

It was dark but not so dark that you couldn't see the man in front. Briggs appeared out of the gloom. 'Ready?' he asked.

'Set, sir,' said Carter, adding to his men, 'OK, off your fannies, this is it.'

The squad crouched in file beside the bank, Hoffman and Petersen at the rear with the BAR, Novak just behind Carter where he could be kept under closer supervision. Carter doubted the Baltimore man's reliability as he suspected anyone who had a faintly criminal background – and Novak, in a moment of unguarded alcoholic haze, had once confessed to working with the 'hoods'. There were signs of movements in the field as the rest of Briggs's platoon led Baker Company forward – Baker Company, that is, less the twenty per cent who were casualties and had not been replaced. The battle which had rumbled in the south all day, momentarily faded to a mutter. The enemy lay still to their front. Traffic noise percolated from the north, heavy from within their own lines and those of the British. Re-entering the line was always forbidding to men of imagination like Briggs and Holmberg – though, for the latter, the night sounds of the country held no terrors. To Novak, however, it was frankly petrifying; he had yet to overcome his townsman's fear of field, hedge and copse: for him an isolated barn induced more fears than the dankest of urban backstreets. And with a townsman's political insight, Novak had sensed Carter's mistrust – and reluctantly had to sympathize: granting loyalty to any man was an act of rare grace for Novak. In fact it surprised him that he was giving the matter such thought, for Carter represented authority and Novak was habitually at odds with that.

They groped through patchy darkness as the moon threw shadows into relief. Landmarks that were familiar from their previous occupation of the line again loomed up. Ahead was the dead tree in ghostly silhouette. Then, suddenly, came the first crack of an explosion, not far off to the left. Almost instantly it was followed by a machine-gun's burp and bullets yack-yacking high, clipping leaves from the trees. 'Down,' cried Carter and Briggs together – and superfluously as the squad dived left and right. Holmberg landed squarely on Novak's back, winding him though insufficiently to prevent an instinctive outburst of xenophobia.

'Jeese, those goddam Limeys. Balled it again.'

11   The Patrol

Patrolling is an art and work, therefore, for the specialist – or so its keenest exponents say. And while it may well be true that its most polished practitioners are born and not made, those who survive for more than a couple of patrols against an experienced enemy are the products of sound training, natural insight and acquired knowledge – as well as being beneficiaries from a lucky star. It is sometimes claimed that the best patrollers have their roots deep in country lore and that the true countrymen are gamekeepers, ghillies, poachers and the like. Perhaps, but not all men such as these are necessarily moulded of that hard fibre which persuades them to bide their time and yet, at a moment of paralysing crisis, aids them in a quick decision, that sort of 'right' choice which makes all the difference between life and death.

Frank Davis, Lieutenant, had demonstrated an innate expertise as a patroller in two years' progressive and hard training on open moors and in the close-hedged fields of England. Some might describe him as a countryman in that he lived, before the Army took him, six miles from Winchester and spent Sundays walking the South Downs. His career had been bounded by an accountant's office in the city, his instincts geared to urban life, his natural inclination that of living deep among bricks and mortar, breathing urban fumes, not agricultural ordure. Yet something in nature's environment helped him to merge with hedgerows, to become adept at stalking an invisible or faintly silhouetted quarry in deepest gloom or bright moonlight, quick to see without being seen in darkness – acquiring, in fact, the gift of silence and the ability to sense his opponent's presence and likely reactions. On training schemes he had learnt to quell the sensations of rising tension by a disciplined confidence, a confidence he had acquired by success, and his ability to out-smart the average opponent. But this had been war-gaming and most of those he had out-smarted were of his own kind – easily out-smarted. In Normandy, against an experienced enemy who was hell-bent on survival, the process of learning had to begin all over again, or so it seemed. During his first and, so far, single patrol he had become strangely aware of an unexpected inner tension that threatened to overcome his self-taught calm. There had been that ugly moment when some German machine-gunner, who apparently could see in the dark, let drive from close range and cut the air with a burst which practically removed his cap-comforter. He could still hear the thud and grunt as a man to his left was hit and killed. Then he had smelt blood for the first time. Luck alone had saved him – the blessed silence from that startling gun followed by metallic wrenching as sweating Germans tried desperately to clear a stoppage in the dark. His patrol had run and reached cover just before the gun fired again. To this moment he could not imagine what had alerted that machine-gunner. Had it been chance or was his own technique at fault?

Of those who would accompany him this night all except Private Cain had shared that first experience: Corporal Parker, stolid and rugged, as expert with fists in a dockland pub brawl in Southampton as with a rifle on the ranges, picking his targets with the dexterity of a darts player; yet unimaginative and quite unappalled by the alarm of that first experience: Trefall and Carver, trouble-seekers from days at school and the recruits' depots; young, single, therefore innocent of responsibilities and ready to take dire risks, not once but several times; forever adjourning in private mutually to question authority with youth's brash assurance: then Bardsley, whose biding introspection isolated him from the others in the section, whose basic common sense did more to restrain the indiscretions of Trefall and Carver than, for instance, Parker; the man who quietly and doggedly refused a 'stripe' but who, when that machine-gun stopped firing, had pronounced the right order: 'Now's the time to go, sir,' long before Davis had sensed the opportunity: finally the new boy – Cain – straight from the reinforcement company but with a good report on patrolling; nonchalantly cool in his first experience of shelling on the last day of 'Goodwood' but seemingly over-confident. It was against Davis's better judgement in selecting him, but there was nobody who seemed any better. Their casualties on Operation 'Goodwood', the loss of staunch, well-evaluated characters had seen to that.

Individually he inspected them and with each found something amiss. Even Parker had pocketed a letter from his wife: 'She'll not know if you leave it behind'. Trefall, with money to chink in his pocket: 'You won't bribe that lot over there'. Carver, with a faulty magazine – castigated at length because it was an old misdemeanour. Bardsley, lacking full facial minstrel-blacking – a trivial error but not to be overlooked. Cain, found correct in every detail until he was discovered to be wearing plimsolls when Davis had specified boots. 'Why?' 'I make too much noise in them, sir. Always did at the Depot.'

'Well this isn't the Depot and what I say goes. Get changed and learn to do as you're told.' A moment later Davis asked himself if that harsh and unpremeditated 'rocket' was fair or wise.

In the fading shreds of daylight they crouched behind the hedge. 'Now remember,' said Davis, 'it's the lane and, most of all, the gateway we're interested in, but first of all, what goes on at the barn. Moon's about right. If we keep close to the bank on the right as we go out there's not much chance of our being seen. I'll lead with Bardsley, Corporal Parker will follow with the others to bail us out if we hit trouble. And for God's sake, Corporal, keep your distance this time so you can do something to help without being pinned if we get caught as before.'

'Sir.'

'You OK now Cain? Well, take it easy as we go and just copy the others. Watch out for mines. No acts of heroism anyone; let's get back in one piece. Perhaps Jerry'll stay quiet, but all that fuss the Yanks have been making on the right may have needled them a bit.'

They fidgeted and fingered equipment, suppressing their fears while Davis spoke with Tim Parsons whose platoon still occupied this sector of hedgerow. Parsons' role was important. It was for him to note the enemy's reaction and stand by to help the patrol if it ran into trouble - not forgetting to observe the niceties of passwords and the precise counting of each returning member. The latter was essential in order to avoid confusion should an enterprising enemy tack on behind to enter the British position unobserved. Garston was there, too, to see them off and check all was well. 'I'll be watching,' he said. 'Take it easy.'

'OK?' said Davis, 'let's go,' and they stepped forward - and

with a single pace became the foremost, lonely elements in Montgomery's 21st Army Group - and all too conscious of the distinction.

Eastwards the guns flashed and squabbled over Caen. Aircraft droned, but that was comforting if it helped drown the rustle of their approach. The Americans were quiet: that officer of theirs said they would try to stay that way - but you could never be sure with other people's armies. The Germans were absolutely still - perhaps there was nobody at the barn. Perhaps not.

A cloud crossed the moon, darkening the scene as they reached the half-way stage to the barn. 'Butterflies' fluttered in Davis's stomach, defying his effort to concentrate harder on the job. He stopped to check bearings and instantly found himself in close company with five men instead of Bardsley. Parker had done it again and drifted in close. The nocturnal stillness of no-man's land inhibits a stentorian parade ground reprimand, but his whisper was tense with anger and disquiet. It was amusing to Bardsley though, as, for one quirkish moment, he recalled to mind a Bairnsfather cartoon from the First World War - Old Bill, on all fours with Bert crawling astern, his bayonet impinged upon Bill's rump, 'I wish the 'ell you'd put a cork on that b- pin of yours, Bert,' it was captioned. This was it. Not that Parker had been aware that he was astray: he dearly longed to lie back, for he never relished taking the lead. But throughout the years he had successfully concealed his principal physical deficiency - a lack of good night vision allied to indifferent direction-keeping ability. The rebuke, therefore, was virtually superfluous and, worse, merely forced him into estimating rather than computing Davis's progress - into keeping distance by guesswork. Trefall and Carver were of no assistance because of his disinclination to ask them for help. Cain was still too overawed to chip in and, in any case, the rebuff over the plimsolls had quenched his initiative.

The barn loomed close, blurred and more gloomily menacing, so it seemed, than when Davis had examined it through binoculars in daylight. He signalled Bardsley to come nearer, observing, in approving detachment, the orthodox leopard crawl executed by his companion - rifle held foremost, head low, buttocks down and legs drawn up. Together they scanned the barn and, beyond, the faint half-tone in the hedge where the enemy post was rumoured to be. They watched and waited, willing a first false move by the enemy – and hoping, too, that Parker would keep distance. This time, in fact, they were saved from his uninvited arrival by Cain who, quick to see Davis stop, had involuntarily cautioned his leader.

Still nothing happened. Davis edged forward again, crawling for the barn's shadow in the hope that, from a fresh angle, the gateway would stand clearly revealed. Also the shadow offered safety, and so they strained towards it. There came a faint 'clunk' from the direction of the gate. They froze – posteriors raised, heads down, warily trying to relate the sound with its source.

It was a bad moment, too, for Oberfusilier Braun. He and Staedler had crept into their camouflaged gun pit an hour before, carrying the MG 34 and its magazines, as they had for three nights past. Here they would stay as outpost until dawn when, as of routine, the position would be evacuated. Stealth was abhorrent to Braun. In a brawl – above all in an attack when winning – exaltation could actually seize him: but this catch-as-catch-can stuff held no enchantment. Moreover he was feeling despondent. Even to his rather dull imagination it was apparent that Germany was losing the war. The bombing, the shelling, the feeling that, away to his left, the Americans had broken through, ate into his confidence. He had no desire that they should draw attention to themselves and was dreadfully fearful already, with the instinct of three years' combat experience, that they were being watched. He checked the freedom of the MG34's ammunition belt. It was this that caused the container to over-balance against the gun. With the noise they too froze.

Davis was tempted. Something was there, but what? It might be enough to return and report what had been heard, though not seen. Yet he knew they ought to investigate closer – his training and conscience demanded that. Ten yards nearer, then another spell in observation, and that would suffice, he reasoned. Two crawls forward, eyes alternately glued to the gate and searching the apertures in the barn which now looked clearer and properly defined - no longer a vague shape. The light improved as the moon emerged from behind its cloud. Then came the click - an innocent snap, yet loaded with deadly significance to the initiated and as deafening as if a gun had been fired from the doorway ahead. The trip wire to the jumping mine, which his hand had brushed, caused a canister to leap high. There came the tearing crump as it burst, 360 steel pellets rending the air. As it exploded he heard Bardsley's gasp. Then all hell was let loose.

Three red flares arched up from somewhere behind the barn - which Parsons and his men recorded for further reference. Braun, careless of seeking an exact target centre, fired a long burst that whistled some eight feet above and to the left of the cowering British patrol. The Americans away to the west, recognizing the familiar crack of an MG 34 and receiving its bullets, threw skyward their own contribution of flares, illuminating the area in stark brilliance and at once filling each shadow with small-arms fire. The Germans, in response to the red alarm flares, chimed in with mortar fire - the usual 81 mm stuff, Parsons judged it to be, that invariably made life uncomfortable for him since its mean-point of impact fell close in front of the double-banked hedge. Nevertheless, this was useful information both to Garston and Culpepper, who, a hundred yards off, were drawing important conclusions.

But, at first, where Davis and Parker crouched low and prayed, constructive reactions were anything but cool or calculating. Davis suffered an urgent desire to jump up and run - all the more so once it was certain that the enemy fire was going high. However, the screen of mortar fire, isolating him from base, and the overriding thought that Bardsley was hit combined to dissuade him. He groped for Bardsley who groaned, 'It's my legs. They're dead. I can't move 'em. What the hell's wrong with them?' A note of panic there which Davis recognized.

'All right, lie still and keep quiet if you can,' whispered Davis soothingly. 'We'll get you out of this somehow.'

He spoke with false confidence and felt horribly lonely. This was the moment when Parker's blundering arrival would have been more than welcome to help remove the incapacitated man. Where the bloody hell was he now?

Parker, in fact, ever the soldier to obey orders to the letter if he possibly could, was deploying his party for the prearranged counter-action – a blast of rifle rife aimed in the general direction of the gate in the pious hope that Davis and Bardsley could make their escape under its cover. It could not have been more perfectly timed. Just as Davis knelt above Bardsley to drag him back the volley roared out and caused him violently to flatten again. From friend and foe a second cascade of flares shot up and the MG 34, spraying wildly, seemed to aim closer.

Davis lost composure. 'Stop bloody firing,' he bawled across his shoulder. It was to no effect. Five rounds' worth had been ordered from each rifle and nobody could hear him above the racket. Then he found Cain by his side, the only man in Parker's group who seemed able to see in the dark and who also had the imagination to divine what was amiss. Together he and Davis pulled and pushed the wincing Bardsley towards the shelter of the hedge, their fear forgotten in the intensity of the mission and the instinctive urge to save life. Parker let them pass, coolly guarding their retreat, waiting for the flares to extinguish. Then suddenly the whole world seemed to go wild as a couple score rounds of American shells hissed down and burst in the field about fifty yards away. That did the trick. The Germans stopped pumping up flares. Braun's MG 34 ceased fire. The darkness enclosed them all, and anxiously Parsons shepherded the patrol to safety through the hedge.

Half an hour later Garston heard Davis's report to Simcox. It confirmed what he and the others had seen and would be reflected in the final plan of attack. Parker, Davis had savagely told Garston, would not patrol again – not with him at any rate. And Garston, registering the haggard expression on Davis's face and the taut pitch to the subaltern's voice, made the private reservation that he who did well in training was not necessarily so good when it came to the real thing. He wondered how long Davis could last, and reflected that the new boy, Cain, had done well. Felix Chandler came over after making a preliminary examination of the injured Bardsley before packing him off to the Advanced Dressing Station. 'Bit early to say,' he replied in answer to Davis's question. 'There's something lodged against the vertebra which is causing paralysis of the lower body and limbs. If it's not gone too far he may be perfectly normal once the thing has been removed. On the other hand there could be permanent damage and in that case he may not walk again.' Davis thanked the doctor and walked across to comfort Bardsley, offering him a cigarette and saying he'd write to his parents.

'You'll have a cushy time at the Depot for a few weeks before we get you back,' he said.

'I'll tell you what it's like,' said Bardsley with a forced smile, 'but they say it's Burma Looms Ahead for those who go back to Blighty. I'd rather come back to the boys if I can.'

'We'll see what can be done,' said Davis, and watched the stretcher bearers lift the wounded man onto the rack of the ambulance jeep.

Private Cain, meantime, was getting ready to sleep, changing from boots into plimsolls. Battle for him had resolved itself into the image of his fancy - a clean-cut, adventurous contest between adversaries from which he, the central hero, emerged unscathed. That earlier experience of bombardment which had left him so unmoved, had been a fine introduction to war. It had failed to harm a single member of the platoon. In his imagination, he relegated shell bursts to the innocuity of battle simulation charges such as were used on schemes in England. He had become somewhat contemptuous of the older men who evinced such fear. It had been he who had kept his head and rescued the wounded man under fire. In Bardsley he recognized the archetype wounded hero, who kept a stiff upper lip and who remained whole - unsoiled by blood, torn flesh or shattered bone. Private Cain, who had yet to see a mangled corpse, was elated.

12 Hammers of Battle

Thomas Pratt, Captain, Royal Artillery, and Adjutant of 203rd Regiment RA sat in the Command Post vehicle surrounded by maps and the apparatus of calculation and power. It was in his hands to control the fire of his regiment's twenty-four 25-pounder guns. What was more he could also help concentrate the fire of every gun in the division, plus the might of 8th AGRA, with a vast outpouring of destruction and terror. For Pratt had access to a network of reliable radio and telephonic communications that covered the entire divisional frontage, reached backwards to the CRA and his staff, where they worked in close accord with the Divisional Commander (and thus farther back still to the Corps Commander and the CCRA), and sideways to the other divisional artillery regiments. Not only could he tap the stream of up-to-the-minute information, which filled these nets with voices, but he forged a vital staff link in directing artillery fire along the frontage of 159th Lorried Infantry Brigade, with the capability of dropping shells on almost any point within an area of thirty square miles. Yet he was merely a cog in a very large wheel, taking instructions either from his Commanding Officer, who stood at the side of the Brigadier, or one of the three battery commanders who acted – as did Culpepper to Simcox – as advisors to infantry or tank COs. Most likely of all, however, he worked under instructions from a trusted forward Observation Officer dug unobtrusively in a commanding position scanning the enemy front. For the past twenty-four hours, in fact, most information had come from the DCBO with priority on counter-mortar work. For the moment, however, there was a pause as the organization readied itself for sustained effort.

Captain Paul Thornton was the FOO watching the front of 1st East Hampshires, detecting, reporting and, sometimes, engaging targets that fell within the authority granted by his CO and limited by the quantity of ammunition available. He enjoyed real power since, in dire emergency, he could call for help, not only from his own battery and the regiment but, by screaming down the radio 'Uncle Target! Uncle Target! Uncle Target!' followed by the essential data, from the fire of every gun in the division – all forty-eight of its 25-pounders. This was not a commonplace event, yet it was at the discretion of Thornton and the other FOOs, founded on the principle of shoot first, discuss afterwards.

This morning Thornton's prime concern was the eight guns of 'P' Battery which, in direct support of the East Hampshires, lay concealed beneath nets in a field some three thousand yards behind the front. His own 'A' Troop, like 'B', its twin in the same battery, was emplaced in an irregular line, its four guns some twenty-five yards apart, their cartridges and shells stacked within reach, ready for the prolonged concentrations soon to be fired. Nearby, parked under trees, stood the prime movers and limbers, ready to dash forward and hook up the guns if some sudden redeployment was demanded. Just now, however, the guns were tied strictly to a defensive role and were intended to remain so until shifting their lay for participation in the attack at 0655 hours. With a long, laborious day ahead of them, each detachment of five under its Sergeant (Number 1) waited at rest. Even so, every gun was loaded, laid on bearing and elevation – responsive to a touch on the firing lever that would dispatch its shell to a pre-arranged point. This was known as an SOS task, designed to deliver an emergency barrage of shells against a predicted zone of likely enemy attack. Crews slept near their guns, snug in freshly dug slit-trenches, though there were gunners on immediate call who squatted behind the gun-shields, ears cocked for SOS orders over the loud-hailers that were connected to the battery command post.

The hour before sunrise is rated among the most threatening of a battlefield day. Then it is that an attacker frequently tries to take advantage of half light (and, perhaps, early morning mist) while ensuring the full span of daylight hours for subsequent activities. At dawn front-line soldiers stiffly rouse and stand shivering to their weapons, impatiently longing for the period of danger to pass and to be allowed to wash, shave and eat. First light on 30th July, delayed by lowering clouds, passed uneventfully in the vicinity of Caumont. The German battalions heaved a sigh of relief, stood down and turned to routine tasks. Not a shot had come from the British lines – to belie the reported threat and the turmoil actually taking place behind them.

Hard at work were the British gunners in their command posts and gun-pits. Final instructions for each phase of the bombardment had arrived during the night and, by first light, had been computed and converted into detailed orders for each gun detachment: detail inscribed on a printed form which laid down the exact time and duration of each period of bombardment, the type of projectile, the charge classification, the range and angle of sight and bearing. The eight gun-commanders of 'P' Battery had been called to the Command Post at 0530 hours to hear their instructions and synchronize their watches, while their men divided the time eating and re-arranging ammunition stacks within the blast walls that were constructed of metal ammunition boxes filled with earth.

Sergeant Henry Bastick cast a bleak eye over his detachment and tersely told Lance-Bombardier Chappell that the shells and cartridges were neither easy to reach nor sufficiently protected by earthworks. Then he settled back against the gun-shield, a greasy bacon sandwich in hand, to study the notes attached to his clip board. He had been told the battery would be firing a linear concentration that started at 0655 hours and continued for forty-five minutes. The range was stated as 7,800 yards, varied on the range scale by local meteorological conditions which, judging by a rising wind, might soon be due for amendment. Good meteor could turn the scales between an accurate and an inaccurate shoot and thus condition the chances of survival for those infantry and tankmen who moved close to the shell's intended point of impact. Each shell's flight was significantly affected by atmospheric and wind conditions that were constantly under review and subject to alteration as the day advanced amid changing weather.

Until 0645 hours his gun was to stand fast on its current SOS bearing. With slight anxiety Bastick registered the silence at the front. He had expected to hear the roar of fighter bombers followed by their distant, screaming dive and the screech of their rockets. Nothing like this was happening and so the absence of the fighter bombers could only enlarge the importance of artillery and his part in the coming attack. The low cloud precluded aerial participation and even now threatened cancellation of the main bomber effort that was scheduled to start two hours after the battle had begun. Thus some targets would remain undisturbed. Nothing, in fact, would unsettle German composure until five minutes before the first man advanced – a gloomy prospect for infantry and tanks. It was hardly likely to paralyse Bastick, however, who was single-mindedly conditioned to perform a familiar task of keeping his men and their gun in action, driving and encouraging the crew to be both accurate and diligent in maintaining their efforts, possibly for hours on end. It always demanded an exhausting level of physical labour, humping shells while their ears and senses were drummed by the roar and crack of the pieces they served, while perennially threatened by sudden retribution from a hostile counter-battery programme.

The hands of his watch crept close to 0645. He glanced at the loudspeaker and turned to his crew. 'Stand-by,' he remarked quietly.

'Take post,' barked the loudspeaker.

'Move,' roared Bastick and the crew jumped – Chappell into the layer's seat, the four ammunition numbers behind the breach; Bastick one hand to the handspike (for traversing), the other thrust into the air as notification to the troop officer, standing in rear, that he was ready – and, as usual, slightly ahead of the other guns in the troop. Bastick was a regular, slower witted, perhaps, than some of these wartime conscripts, who were in the majority in this troop, but proud of his ability to excel them all in a drill movement.

'Battery Target, Stonk,' came the troop commander's call. 'HE 177. Charge 3. Angle of Sight, 15 minutes. Elevation, Zero 171 degrees 25 minutes. Fire by order. Number 1, 7800; Number 2, 7850, Number 3, 7875; Number 4, 7925' – those were the ranges for each individual gun.

At each order Bastick carefully supervised his men's performance. Chappell (the Number 3) set Charge 3 on the range-scale plate, then the angle of sight on the clinometer (Bastick moving sideways from his place at the gun's trail to check that the setting was correct); then the bearing which, in this case, required no major adjustment since, by chance, the gun was already pointing in roughly the right direction; and finally range for elevation. Each phrase from the troop commander was acknowledged by Bastick with hand in air. On receipt of '7800', he concentrated on watching Chappell make fine adjustments to clinometer, bringing its bubble steady, levelling the cross sights, aligning cross wires in his telescope on the aiming mark, followed by a fine downward adjustment to level exactly the clinometer bubble. Last of all, with a slap on his backside, Chappell indicated to Bastick that, so far as he was concerned, all was ready.

Meantime the others had been through the oft-repeated loading drill: Number 4 presenting the shell to the breach, Number 2 forcing it home with thrust of a short ramrod, Number 5 turning to take the next shell, proferred by Number 6 (who worked at the ammunition stack). Then Number 4 seized a brass cartridge case from Number 5 and showed the contents to Bastick so he could verify that the charge inside was right. 'Correct,' cried Bastick as permission for Number 4 to put on the lid, thrust case behind shell into breach until the extractors tripped and the breach block rose. At once Number 2, breach lever in hand and feeling the jump, rotated the lever until the breach closed, while Number 4 took the next shell from Number 5. An all-embracing glance and Bastick raised his hand again, shouting, 'Ready'.

Again he was first, the job complete and true in less than a hundred seconds, the other Number 1s, seconds later, reporting until the troop commander could tell the battery command post,

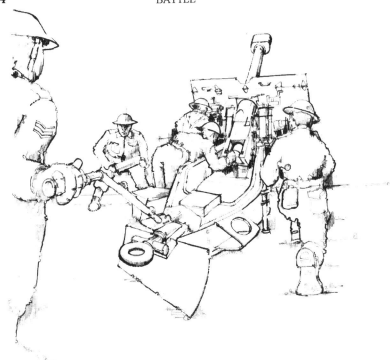

' 'A' Troop ready' and Battery could report 'Ready' over the wireless to the Adjutant.

Minutes hung heavily as H hour approached; the Adjutant, microphone poised; the battery command posts alert; troop commanders eager and layers with hand on firing lever. At last: 'Hullo All Stations One. Fire.' 'All Stations, fire,' repeated Battery. 'Fire,' shouted the troop commanders. 'Number One! Fire!' yelled Bastick.

Philip Snow's squadron stood-to in the seclusion of the orchard that served as their Forming Up Place. They had moved there slowly and mutedly under low revving engines in the fading hours of darkness. Beneath nets thrown casually across turrets and hull they awaited the dawn. All around, in orchards and lanes, had growled a well-ordered activity to contrast favourably and confidently with the undermining chaos of the previous night on the roads approaching Caumont. Wireless silence had officially been broken at 0355 hours, though there had been no need to transmit emergency messages. They had watched groups of infantry ambling by in file and now saw sappers clearing a minefield by the subdued light of torches. They had become chilled in the night air and felt the oncoming queasy-stomached apprehension of fear.

When the leading strands of light tinted the clouds at 0515 hours Snow nodded to Sergeant Bearstead on the other side of the turret. 'OK, check net,' he ordered.

Pad on knee, pencil in one hand and microphone in the other, Bearstead pressed the pressel switch and called in the high-pitched straining voice that was trade-mark of the best radio operators, obtaining, too, the optimum performance from Amplitude Modulated radio sets:

'Hullo all stations Tare 1. Report my signals. All stations Tare 1, over.'

A pause and the entire squadron, all 'netted' to the same frequency, began its reply in order of precedence with varying quality – all, that is, less those operators who had overlooked that a net check was scheduled. One by one the harsh replies sounded through Bearstead's headset, each accompanied in headphones by a growling heterodyne rumble or whistle as he thumbed the netting button as a test against the tuned accuracy of each outstation.

'Hullo Tare 1, Hullo Tare 1. OK, over,' replied the operator of Number 1 troop leader, the slightest growl in Bearstead's headset indicating an almost perfect tuning.

'Hullo Tare 2, Hullo Tare 2. Strength three Tare 2, over,' but this one was accompanied by a high-pitched whistle to explain both its fainter reception and the off-net condition of the set. And so on until all had answered and Bearstead had ticked them on his list before calling for remedial action from those off-net. Snow climbed ponderously from the turret to greet his assembled troop officers.

'A lousy net,' he grumbled. 'Andrew,' turning to 2 Troop's leader. 'Yours way off. Grip it when you get back.' He paused to let his remonstrance sink in. 'OK, now we've not much time, but just enough, I hope, to go to the crest up there and see what little's to be seen of where we're going. I doubt, though, if there'll be time for your other commanders to have a look, but we'll see.'

He had given them orders at midnight in the Assembly Area and they had studied the map. That was no substitute for an examination of the ground, however. They had not met their accompanying infantry yet, since only this minute were the leading companies arriving in the Forming Up Place to be greeted by Captain Fred Parrott, Snow's Second-in-Command. His task, as Liaison Officer, was to introduce each company to its affiliated troop of tanks in the initial assault, merely to establish recognition on the pious assumption that understanding of each other's difficulties was solved by basic training. Parsons, from the Gleneagles, was there too, doubting the wisdom of his men being committed to help the East Hampshires. Simcox had been most persuasive with somebody.

'Now, watch it,' warned Snow as they approached the hedge. 'Jerry can see this hedge from the other side.'

They peered through gaps in the foliage at the distant crest, detecting random and indistinct topographical features buried in *bocage*, dimly associating them with the map's intricate detail. The best that could be done in such claustrophobic and time-constricted conditions was to recognize a few prominent features which might provide each troop leader with sufficient orientation and direction. All Snow could do then was leave them to their own conclusions and plans. To right and left Snow observed, and fumed at, the infantry's officers carrying out a parallel task. It worried him that so high a proportion of key leaders should thus be converging on so small a space at once. They were all highly vulnerable if the enemy saw them and laid down fire.

He curtailed his own officers' investigations and led them back to the tanks, discussing plans as they went - the need to maintain good communications with the infantry (a bold suggestion, as one experienced troop officer remarked); the desirability of keeping within close support of each other and of 'brassing up' the hedges with machine-gun fire as they advanced in order to intimidate German bazooka parties; the avoidance of mines as yet undetected; the advisability of loading the main armament with a high-explosive shell (for general area effect) or with armour-piercing shot as a pin-point anti-tank weapon. Most troop officers plumped for high explosive and nominated just one of their tanks for armour-piercing tasks, relying on the Firefly troop with its 17-pounder guns to deal with enemy tanks.

Conferences between infantry and tank crews were taking place in the FUP as each infantryman was shown the identification marks on individual tanks, and as infantry wireless operators 'netted' their sets to the tanks' infantry-type sets. Platoon and troop leaders met to confirm the system of visual signalling that would be used to indicate targets to each other. It might be by shouting, if a tank commander could be persuaded to leave his turret or an infantryman would dare climb up, or it might be by wave of hand. Nobody placed much reliance on radio talk because the infantry sets were notoriously fickle and their owners unlikely to use them out of lack of confidence in their efficiency. Much more faith was placed in older, tried methods – the firing of tracer ammunition or a Verey flare towards a target to indicate its location. By mutual, if unspoken, consent it was agreed that no one method was foolproof, though there was always a chance that one type or another might answer in an emergency.

The time crept closer to 0655. Tank crews were returning, shovels in their hands, from nearby thickets – the disposal of Nature's waste was to be accomplished before, rather than during, action into a shell-case inside the turret. Infantry, crouching low, watched the tank crews climb aboard – drivers and co-drivers closing hatches, and commanders, last into the turret, pulling steel helmets over headsets. Each tank's essential, pre-battle tests were already done. All were as mechanically ready as ever they would be. At the same moment as the artillery regiments in rear swung their guns against the new targets, tank commanders in the FUP gave the final order of committal.

'Action!'

Loaders swung open main armament breach block, selected a round of ammunition and thrust it home until the rim tripped the extractors, closing the breach automatically. Belts of machine-gun ammunition were dragged from their boxes, threaded into the Brownings that were then cocked twice.

'Loaded,' came the cry in eighteen turrets – and again they waited, some smoking, a few talking softly. This was the sacred moment when praying men asked help of their God, while even those innocent of the religious habit explored some special form of comfort. Sergeant Angus Grant, a Presbyterian, reflected, head rising from chest, that a visit in the FUP from the padre might not have been amiss (it was Sunday after all) and recalled, with satisfaction, how his entire crew, prior to 'Goodwood', had been in the habit of pre-battle prayer. He hoped the new man, Armstrong, was similarly inclined – otherwise he might not be so good in action! As it happened Armstrong had not failed them and now he was all eagerness, scanning through the narrow field of his periscope and glancing sidelong at Brown, sitting impassively in the driver's seat, chewing a hardtack biscuit. Armstrong realized, with a little surprise, that his major consideration, apart from apprehension, was of curiosity. What would be his reactions now that the real thing was imminent? By the end of the day a number of personal problems might be solved, he thought.

From afar came the bong of a foot-loose gun, but before the twitter of its passing shell there was an enraged volley which rifled the air and then tore it to shreds above them.

'Start up,' said Grant in his tank-park voice.

13 Bombardment

Walking at a stiff pace, steel helmet in hand and cap at the regulation angle, Jurgen Irkens arrived at the crest's rim where the long 75mm anti-tank gun in its pit overlooked and guarded the approaches to Vertefeuille Farm. It was his habit to inspect at least one or other of the company locations every morning, not so much with the intention of finding fault, though his eye was constantly in search of things which might be done to improve the defences, but as a demonstration of his presence and an exercise in personal leadership. He had visited the crew of the sleek Jagdpanther, hidden deep in a thicket behind the crest, and found the crew in a temper over an article in the magazine *Signal* slanging a writer whose journalistic enthusiasm had confused the tank force with the artillerymen who manned self-propelled guns such as theirs. Theirs was a parochial pride which Irkens respected if only because of the healthy competitive spirit it engendered. Yet he twitted them.

'I find it difficult to see the difference between the tankmen and yourselves sometimes myself,' he said and laughed at their chorus of remonstrance. 'Anyway, keep your rage for the Americans,' he added.

Solemnly Unteroffizier Pankewitz patted the long 88mm gun protruding from its mantlet in the smooth glacis plate.

'This is all we need, sir,' he had said. 'This and plenty of ammunition.'

When the first shells began to fall Irkens spared a thought for

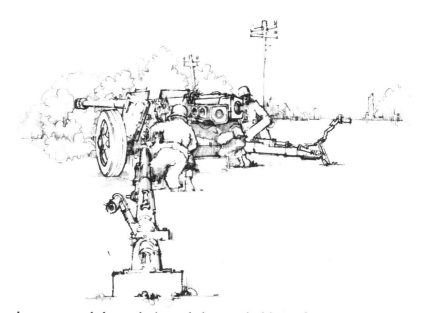

that crew and devoutly hoped that, as holders of the best trump card in hand, it was already safely behind armour. There was no further time for serious reflection. His place was back at the command post. Yet a hasty retreat must not lead to misinterpretation by the men. All around the enemy were creating terror. Beyond the crest the farm was erupting in livid flashes, spouting geysers of smoke and dust. The hedges to right and left were obscured by the deluge of enemy shells. This was the real thing – no mere bout of local harassing fire. The entire divisional frontage, he could tell by the merging sounds, was engulfed in a full-scale bombardment as intense as any he had experienced. Shells were dropping behind him too – somewhere among the artillery bunkers, no doubt – and superimposed, close by, was the sigh and seductive plop of mortar bombs which belched white smoke to generate impenetrable fog. And now, too, high explosive was being mixed with the smoke bombs that bounced through the copse, introducing a sequence of rending crashes and driving, screaming splinters that scarred tree trunks and cut down branches and leaves in profusion. He retraced his footsteps, cheerfully calling encouragement to the 75mm gun crew where it cringed: strolling away (while fighting the temptation to run and lose dignity) and glancing left to see, with satisfaction, the Jagdpanther's hatches closing. Older comrades who saw him recalled his record as a leader and felt no qualms that he was deserting them, but the newcomers were disturbed and the malcontents complained: 'There he goes. One whiff of danger and back to the bunker!'

In Vertefeuille Farm Oberfeldwebel Walter Kramer had barely finished a routine telephone report to Obergefreiter Hauser. 'Nothing to report,' he had said and replaced the receiver. At that moment the first shell arrived, removing the kitchen chimney stack, and almost immediately a deluge followed, shaking the building to its foundations with concussions that sucked the breath from his lungs. Walls cracked and bulged, rafters shifted and fell, but these things appeared to Kramer as an inconsequential kaleidoscopic effect that was completely secondary to his clear-cut intention to survive. He plunged sideways towards the nearest substantial cover under the stairway. Looking back, he watched a great oak beam whirl through the room, saw the kitchen table with its canteens and food collapse, and registered, with astonishment, young Leutnant Frimmel striding purposefully through the flying debris, bent on some incomprehensible mission. It was all over in a flash. The chunk of bursting shell ripped the officer in half, his segments barely held together by clothing, his remains almost instantly covered by a heavy fall of plaster. Grimly Kramer recorded that, should he survive the bombardment, command of the so-called *'Graben'* position had fallen upon him. Somehow this realization re-dedicated his professional attitude and partly assuaged the terror. He began to give some groping thought to his companions.

Those in the cellar felt lucky, though terrified that the exits might become blocked, while the ones in deep trenches dug amidst the farmyard perhaps felt safest of all: at least their lungs were not choked by dust. Some unfortunate fusiliers had been caught in the open and were compelled to hug the ground and crawl slowly towards the nearest hole, their sense of direction gradually overcome by obscuration from dust in a changing landscape. Pummelled into semi-consciousness by the roar of discharge, men clutched themselves and each other in fear, their cheeks pale from shock. It was inevitable that some of the weaker members should collapse in nervous exhaustion. In a moment of abject distraction, one of them leapt from his trench to race blindly through the maelstrom and, as a providential example to the others, was cut down instantly, flung against a wall in a pulverized bundle of flesh, bone and clothing.

By chance Oberfusilier Braun, dozing contentedly in a dugout cut deep into the bank overlooking the scene, was a smug spectator. He had retired from his night post and the barrage had awoken him, of course. Its epicentres avoided his comrades and himself, however, striking to left and right and far in rear. They peeped coyly above the rim of the ditch to watch in awe and fear, to hear a sound like a gigantic kettle boiling, and sense the rapid alterations in atmospheric pressure that battered their ears. Freakishly they became mesmerized, suspended in isolation from the holocaust.

Yet from this temporary sanctuary, they had the opportunity to observe, undistracted, what was going on before them. Suddenly they perceived objects and people in motion. Domed shapes had appeared on the distant crest line and a tank pushed through the far hedge and headed down the slope into the valley. Here and there came men, too, some ambling and some running, their destination, apparently, the farm. Neither Braun nor his comrades were the swiftest of thinkers; moreover, as infantrymen – the battlefield's most vulnerable mortals – they had come to rely for salvation on all other kinds of weapons before making use of their own! Therefore, although these scurrying, hostile figures were ideal targets for their machine-gun and rifles, they did not at once open fire, preferring to wait, instead, for somebody else to act – for the artillery and mortars to fire, the tanks to shoot. But for different reasons nobody else reacted and the vulnerable targets slipped from view and took cover in the hedgerow bounding the lane.

Why this slow German reaction? Why did they not carpet the approaches with their SOS fires when the British infantry appeared and before it could pass through the zone of interdiction? Partly to blame was the density of *bocage* that restricted the Germans' observation as severely as that of their opponents. While Braun had been privileged in enjoying so comprehensive a view, von Schilling, in his look-out, had not only been surprised by the suddenness of the bombardment, but doubly unsighted both by the foliage covering the British frontage and the smoke and dust that rapidly prevented him from observing more than a dozen metres ahead. Nevertheless he did not see SOS signal lights ascending from the foremost troops as the call for defensive fire because none, in fact, were fired. A brief disjointed sentence on the telephone from an excited orderly in the left flank position divulged nothing and broke off when the cable was severed by a shell burst.

An important reason for the British passing unchallenged into the comparative safety of the German forward zone (where combat could only be man against man, divorced from the bullying dominance of heavy, indirect fire weapons) was the pace of their charge compressed into the brief space of two minutes that elapsed between the last shell falling and the time it took the leading East Hampshires to cross open ground and reach the Germans in the lane beyond.

In the interest of control and composure, infantry moves towards combat at a measured gait, rather as a policeman approaches crime. They rise from the ground and advance in precise formation, weapons held at the ready, hoping thereby to come to the grapple in decent order, attempting, in fact, to postpone the inevitable confusion of individual combat for as long as possible. This was the prescribed drill – and Lieutenant Harry Spriggs had been hard-pressed to persuade his Company Commander, John Codrington, that drills, like rules, are made to be circumvented.

'You can't just sprint across eighty yards and hope to arrive in trim the other side,' objected Codrington when Spriggs proposed this course. 'The men will be in a muck-sweat, their formation lost, their hands trembling so they'll not shoot straight when they get there.'

'To take your last point first,' retorted his subordinate, 'how often do they shoot and what do they hit if they do? And with regard to formation – well, unless we're across that bloody pasture before a stonk comes down we'll never get across at all – in arrow head, line, file or any other order you care to name.

Sorry, sir, but I think you're wrong.'

Thus spoke Codrington's subaltern – but a man to be heeded, for Spriggs was an ex-company sergeant-major whose experience included the coaching of men like Codrington when they were junior officers and who, as a pre-war regular, rather despised Territorials for the amateurs he took them to be.

Codrington had demurred but finally given way. So it was that Spriggs led his men by a carefully concealed route to take post, unseen behind the hedge, eighty yards short of the lane that was their designated objective. There they waited for 0655 hours, cringing as the shells roared and rushed close above their heads to crush the farm. Some landed a mere twenty yards to their front, a splinter nicking the helmet of an inquisitive young private soldier who raised himself to relish the scene. Spriggs knelt on one knee apart from the platoon, ten yards behind the hedge, his radio operator in attendance, and marked closely the three section commanders crouched among their men. From long training he felt sure they were watching him for the start signal. His watch said that the artillery concentration must soon stop. Hand held high he saw, with satisfaction, the section commanders' hands raised in acknowledgement. There came the scheduled slackening of the gunfire. Yet he paused just a fraction of a minute to be safe – a well-rewarded precaution as four last-second shells roguishly burst in the field beyond.

His hand dropped and he leapt to his feet shouting loudly, 'Go on you silly bastards,' running to breast the hedge where the boldest spirits among the platoon scrambled through. The scene before was hung brown and white in smoke, the distant hedge spasmodically visible in murk. To right and left the platoon struggled into view until enough were committed in the open to be assured of a strong gathering on the objective. Only then did Spriggs run forward again towards the enemy, fairly confident that the others would follow. He knew of instances in other units when the officer's lead had not been followed. He'd look silly arriving in solitary splendour in the German lines. Even ex-sergeant-majors have a dignity to maintain. But men were more scared of him than of the enemy.

This was what Braun had seen and allowed to happen

unchallenged, the rush which caught five bewildered German fusiliers deep underground still taking shelter from the shells. In less than five minutes Spriggs's platoon was completely in possession of its company's first objective, Spriggs firing a Verey pistol aloft with a red-over-green success signal, barking orders to his men to re-organize. Codrington, who had watched through the lower branches of a tree, anxiously supervising the other platoons marching towards the farm, observed six grey figures detach themselves from 'Spriggs's hedge' to stumble back. These were the evidence of success – prisoners and escort.

With a sigh and a succession of rending crashes the German mortar DF landed squarely among the prisoners and the rest of the company, isolating Spriggs and his men by smoke and flying metal. Across a narrow front belched instantaneous explosions that enveloped stumbling soldiers in a phantasmagoria of billowing, flame-specked clouds. Codrington witnessed a handful of the Gleneagles platoon somehow break free and throw themselves wildly beneath the far hedge of the lane; watched his own men and the second echelon of Gleneagles wilt and fade – falling where they stood, scattering or, like the hapless group of prisoners, caught midway and converted to rags and tatters that twitched and died in a shambles.

For five awful minutes the mortars played and when at last they stopped and shaken survivors began to crawl away it was to allow a mere half dozen men to move irresolutely towards the enemy while the rest staggered back in bewilderment. And now the crump of bombs was supplanted by the crackle of bullets scything the field. Braun and his companions had taken courage, and, like hyenas after a killing by lions, were picking off the survivors.

14 The Farm

The first hint of trouble reached Philip Snow through his headphones - the excited voice of 3 troop leader, John McBain, calling.

'Hullo Tare 3! Our friends are across the first field but a colossal stonk's come down and the rest of their lot have had it. Over.'

'Hullo Tare 3,' replied Snow, as slowly and deliberately as he could. 'Now take it easy. See if you can get something across to join the yeomen who've got through. Tell me, too, where they are so we don't shoot them up from here. Over.'

'Hullo Tare 3. Wilco, but all our chaps have bunked. It's hectic, but I'll shove forward best I can. Over.'

Already Snow was telling his driver to change position in order to obtain a better view of Vertefeuille Farm through the upper fringe of the hedge.

'Tare 3. Roger,' he replied, and then, 'Out to you. Hullo Tare 1. Get as close behind 3 as you can when he shifts forward. And keep a bloody sharp lookout. Over.'

'Hullo Tare 1. Wilco, Out,' came the acknowledgement in an exaggerated drawl from Robertson, the new officer. Along the hedgerows engine revs rose high as tanks adjusted their positions in response to Snow's orders.

Snow managed to manoeuvre to where he could see a slightly larger segment of the ground surrounding the farm, and in so doing hazardously exposed his tank's hull to the crest on the right. But he noticed one of the Fireflies poke its long gun through the hedge to his right and hoped well of this friendly support.

Three troop leader, in company with the tank under command of a corporal, burst through the hedge and entered the heart of the German counter bombardment, moving as fast as the drivers could coax their engines, lurching among shallow craters and the tattered remnants of the dead. They arrived scared but safe, though McBain narrowly missed crushing a petrified East Hampshire cowering in long grass. But his troop corporal, steering sharply to the left, was a few yards short of the lane when smoke and earth belched beneath the tank's forefoot and she yawed to a halt. Anxiously McBain studied the stricken machine - it looked like a mine strike though it might be something worse.

'Tare 3 Baker. Bumped a mine, but we're OK. Over,' came his corporal's terse voice after a pause. As double reassurance the corporal waved from the turret.

McBain was in a dilemma. That mine would be one of many, not an isolated example. There were enemy in the farm and to go there, lacking close infantry escort, would be suicidal. There was little or no chance of infantry reinforcements arriving. Therefore he had to make contact with the only platoon which had got through. But how? So far he had seen only one of them. The rest and their platoon leader were nowhere in sight, though, as he peeped cautiously above the cupola rim, he began gradually to detect crouching khaki figures, some lying still while others fired spasmodically in the general direction of the farm. McBain did not want to dismount, thus sacrificing the safety of armour, but he doubted if an infantryman would come to him, so he took a deep breath, pulled off headsets and dropped into the lane, where, to his astonishment, he met Spriggs. 'That's a stroke of luck,' he remarked. 'I was looking for you.'

'Well, I was hardly likely to climb atop that thing of yours,' came the discomforting answer. 'But I'm mighty glad to see you, too. Look, there's Hun dug into that farm all over the place. What's more there are mines - stacks of 'em. Couple of my blokes caught it over on the left just ahead of that other tank of yours. There'll be more.'

'You can be sure of another thing, too,' said McBain. 'We're solo. Rest o'your company's caught a proper packet. What do you want to do?'

'Well, we can't stay here,' said Spriggs. 'They'll give me stick if I do. Bound to have this lane taped. I've tried to get through on the 38 set but nothing doing. I'd feel safer in the right-hand corner of the farm if possible and then see what happens. Can you come too?'

McBain peered gingerly through the foliage and examined the corner of the farm where it stood so close and yet so far. To the right lay open ground and Heaven alone knew what by way of enemy anti-tank guns sweeping it. He guessed, however, that he might possibly poke through his gun and give fire support over the infantry's heads without exposing too much of his tank. He explained what he had in mind.

'OK,' said Spriggs dubiously. 'It'll take me half an hour to get my chaps ready. Can you tell my OC through your set what goes on? And for God's sake try to join me in the farm as soon as you can.'

'Better than that. I'll try to fix up an artillery shoot to cover our flanks. I'll also get my other tank up to add support. But don't expect me in the farm behind you immediately, though I'll do what I can later.'

They parted, Spriggs to crawl laboriously among his men giving instructions for the next rush forward; McBain to report the situation over the wireless and call forward his sergeant's tank, along with instructions that it was to come up on his right and add fire to the advance on the farm.

'Tare 3. OK,' said Snow as the troop officer completed his call. 'I'll get Sheldrake to keep the pot boiling and stop him firing on the farm just before your friends move in. Call Sign 1 will give all the help he can and so will I, but there's not much we can see in the foreground. Out to you, Hullo 1, Hullo 4. Acknowledge and stand by to support 3 as he goes in. Over.'

Now began the process of adjusting the artillery fire to suit the revised infantry plan on the left and bring the reserve troops into play. Brian Culpepper, eavesdropping on the tank wireless net, was passing instructions down the gunner net, and Paul Thornton, the FOO, was getting ready to control that fire. Simcox was digesting news of 'C' Company's obliteration on the left and facing up to the realities of a situation such as had been feared by both Codrington and himself. He hoped that Spriggs might well infiltrate closer to the farm but realized it was hardly likely he could take it. What else was to be done? And what of Codrington himself?

The immolation of his company had been harrowing for Codrington. Of those who had crawled or bolted to safety from the mortar fire there were few upon whom he could rely at once, and little that could be done to throw them back into the fight. It was nearly an hour before he realized that, for a start, all the officers were missing. Accompanied by his sergeant-major he moved among the survivors, trying to re-establish coherence, starting to steady the stalwarts, the brave and the unimaginative – at best attempting to build one platoon out of what, sixty minutes before, had been three. Over the 18 Set he spoke to Simcox who seemed better briefed about Spriggs's platoon than was Codrington – but it was satisfying to hear that part, at least, of his company was still in action. He had always striven to make his company the best in the battalion. They said he coddled it. Perhaps so. Perhaps he was too much the benign father, too little the martinet like Spriggs. He had come, even, to doubt his own beliefs when, two days previously, a soldier of his had virtually denied their purpose at war. With the task of defeating the Germans seemingly hardly begun in France, this man had actually come to enquire when they might be getting leave at home in England – and had seemed surprised when Codrington had angrily discounted any such happening. That man's aims, he disgustedly knew, were to get home – nothing less, and they were disturbingly in opposition to his own purity of purpose, his belief in a dedicated war aim.

'Sergeant-major,' he called. 'Get the wounded to the Aid Post as soon as you can. Then take command of the rest and we'll go to the farm as quickly as we can.'

'Sir,' bawled Company Sergeant-major Huskinson, narrowly avoiding saluting and thus compromising the identity of himself and his leader to any watching enemy sniper. He turned brusquely to the men standing or lying round about him:

'Right you men there! Stand up, let's be having you. You're bloody idle, that's what. Let's see the soldiers among you.'

They stirred and looked sheepishly at him with a mixture of amazement, distaste, fear and respect. This was the personality who for two years past had alternately harried them and taught the basic tricks of their trade, the disciplinarian who, in action, had not slackened his grip one jot and yet, by some miracle of understanding, had bent the rigidity of an inflexible code to an innate humanitarianism, seeming to sense their fears and doubts without once allowing those instincts free rein. They stood up with slow uncertainty as Huskinson strode among them. To a lightly wounded sergeant he addressed his first order. 'You there, Sergeant Shankly, take those wounded men back and see the stretcher bearers miss none of them. Get yourself dressed too.' He barely waited for acknowledgement but swung upon the uninjured. 'Fall in in three ranks, NCOs on the right, Bren gunners on the left. Move now, smartly.'

Their reactions quickened to his familiar bark. It occurred to one or two of them that the concept of adopting a parade-ground formation, practically within sight of the enemy, was ludicrous, but they kept their thoughts to themselves and fell in with the rest. Within their three ranks he assembled twenty armed soldiers and selected three sections commanded by the best NCOs in sight – men he knew could be trusted, one of whom was only a lance-corporal, a bare nineteen years of age, but strong and intelligent.

'Right then. You're Number 10 platoon, you are,' he said. 'And I'm your platoon leader. So now we'll get sorted out in ten minutes flat and get on with the war. Section leaders! Carry on!'

All whirr and track-slap, the carriers were arriving with stretchers, taking aboard the pale and broken wounded – men who were yellow from shock, streaked red where fresh blood contrasted vividly in a tangle of khaki and flesh. Carrier by carrier they returned to the farm where the 'O' Group had been held. Felix Chandler and his orderlies of the Aid Post took over, applying essential first-aid to supplement the bright antiseptic yellow field or shell dressings, administering morphine to those who needed it and who bore no marks of having received it at the front; documenting and, with the help of the padre who moved quietly among them offering cigarettes and words of encouragement, preparing them for the next stage of their journey to the Casualty Collecting Post a mile distant. 'How quiet they always are,' murmured the padre to Chandler. 'Thank God,' replied the doctor, easing a dressing from a leg so badly shattered that plainly it would be amputated within the next few hours. The man winced and fearfully asked, 'OK, sir?'

'You'll do, son. Have you straight in no time.' He replaced the dressing, injected morphine, and annotated the man's card with this information to prevent somebody else later doubling the dose with fatal results. Then he went to the next. 'He's 'ad it, sir,' said the orderly. So they turned to the next.

The thunder of battle rolled over Chandler's small group at the Aid Post. They hardly heard it and somehow found repose by concentrating upon human salvage, along with occasional inspiration from the fortitude of the sufferers and disgust at the waste.

In Vertefeuille Farm there were neither facilities nor time for care of the German wounded and little chance of their evacuation since the enemy artillery barrage prevented their retreat. Furiously increasing small-arms fire came from the front where, Oberfeldwebel Kramer felt pretty sure, a tank had reached the farm's outskirts. Upon this he had now to concentrate his attention, shutting his eyes and ears to those who cried with pain and had no further part to play in the defence. The medical orderly had survived and was hunting through wreckage, carrying his satchel of dressings and drugs from one case to another. He removed a helper from the orderly – a man with but a scratch on his face. 'You'll survive,' he said. 'There's other matters to attend to now. Join Obergefreiter Zeisen in the outhouse bunker over there.'

Kramer was hazily trying to assess his company's strength and match it to the requirements of all-round defence of a position that was already partly dominated by the enemy; trying to discover the gaps caused by casualties and find survivors from the ruins of the tattered garrison to fill them. He searched among broken rafters and masonry, bending low to avoid presenting a target to an unseen foe, grateful that the shelling had stopped yet fearful that this was but the prelude to a direct assault by enemy infantry. He had lost all sense of time, was insensitive to the knowledge that the position was hopeless: he was just grimly determined to engage in what had become the seemingly endless feature of his adult life – combat. The responsibility of command acted as a stimulant and reduced the impact of fear. A truly brave man, in that he had to force himself each time to risk leaving cover, he nevertheless was absorbed by the demands of the moment. Gradually he began to find unwounded soldiers who retained the dregs of resolve: by sharp orders and extrovert example he injected them with his own determination until slowly they began to follow his lead. A patch-work pattern of defence began to take shape in the gratuitous period allowed him by Spriggs, when the latter was forced, also, to spend time substituting a new plan for the one which had collapsed under German mortar fire.

Implacably Kramer and Spriggs began to discover each other's merits as they matched their wits in battle.

The shelling of the farm had hardly ceased when the air became thick with machine-gun bullets, swishing and cracking. Long bursts from a belt-fed gun, noted Kramer, and therefore likely to come from a tank and not the magazine-fed, British Bren LMG. It was an opportune moment to draw that deduction for he had just met Hengst, the panzerfaust man – and still carrying his drainpipe-like weapon, what was more. 'Stay with me,' he demanded and then flinched from a flash in the hedge to their front and a shell bursting close by that covered them with dust. A tank – no doubt about it. 'Can you get him, Hengst?'

'Too far,' replied Hengst. 'Never hit him there.' Anyway neither he nor Kramer had much faith in the rocket weapon, whose potential seemed more improbable than true, so Kramer did not argue.

'Wait and see if he comes closer,' but the words were hardly out of Kramer's mouth when khaki figures emerged from the

hedgerow and ran closer. There was just time to fire once with his sub-machine gun and see somebody drop. There came the bark of grenades near the corner of the farm, shouts, a scream – and silence. Kramer swore. They had broken in all too easily and cheaply. That tank was bound to move next.

'Hengst, give that damn thing to me.'

He seized the panzerfaust and crawled to a gap in the stonework, thrust it through and aimed at the tank whose turret's shape he could distinguish in the foliage, where flashes darted from its machine-gun. Only once before had he fired this unreliable weapon. It was a difficult shot. He placed his trust in luck and loosed-off. There was a bright flash near the target: it looked as if he might have scored a hit though he could not be sure. Nor could he wait to find out, for at once bullets arrived from all quarters. When next he looked the tank had disappeared. Well, it had not advanced and that was what mattered.

McBain had been lucky. The panzerfaust had narrowly missed his turret and exploded among branches; the only casualty was Spriggs's wireless operator who, while standing alongside, had taken its full blast. Spriggs was shaken but the set was irreparably damaged and the operator dead. It took an enormous effort on Spriggs's part to force himself forward to the farm – particularly now he guessed the tank was unlikely to follow. And when he reached the building it was to find a mere handful of his soldiers deep in a dugout in company with a dead and a wounded German – the latter the object of close scrutiny and already the poorer by his watch.

At Vertefeuille Farm, where the situation was one of stalemate, the contenders had demonstrated courage and the ability to give and take fire. Neither comprehended each other's strength, let alone that of their own side in the immediate vicinity: both felt weak – weaker than was desirable for attack or counter-attack. Kramer dully realized it was his duty to hold on. Spriggs felt content to have achieved as much as could be expected of him, though bracing himself to advance again should the enemy show signs of weakening or if that tank arrived. But McBain felt convinced no glory awaited him here. He and his sergeant were snug in the lane, behind its hedgerow, and could keep the farm under fire. To advance was suicidal since, even though the rest of the squadron was committed to his support, their direct help was denied by the obscuration of the *bocage*. In effect, frightened men faced men in fear and looked elsewhere for the resolution of an apparently intractable dilemma.

15 Merging with *Bocage*

Number 3 Platoon in 'A' Company heaved an incredulous sigh of relief when it reached the lane to the right of the barn unscathed. They had crossed the open field in impeccable arrow-head formation at a measured pace in copy-book style. Not a hostile shot had been fired. Their three tanks had maintained a most comforting rattle of machine-gun fire, systematically combing the hedge, the barn and the orchard to the right, and already three additional tanks were bustling to join them while the rest of the company approached in file. It was a most orderly scene that was in complete contrast to the chaos scourging their comrades in 'C' Company to the left and it was largely because on their front the counter-battery bombardment had done its work almost to perfection. The German heavy mortars had been hard hit and their artillery was engaged against the other sectors. Moreover, because Davis's patrol had discovered the hostile machine-gun nest and minefield to the left of the barn, 'A' Company's thrust had been diverted farther to the right, even at peril of falling in too close proximity to the wing of the American bombardment. At any moment now the Americans were due to open fire on the orchard.

Andrew Partridge had agreed a joint plan with 'A' Company. No sooner had the leading section taken the lane and the follow-up section arrived, than he would push through a single tank to dominate the boundary lane on the right while the infantrymen moved in close consort, dealing with enemy who

115

might be there. This would coincide with the American bombardment as it pulverized the orchard while, as they hoped, the enemy's attention was fixed on Vertefeuille Farm. Partridge watched the second platoon arrive, received a wave from its commander and spoke to Sergeant Grant over the wireless. 'Hullo Tare 2 Able. Alright, off you go. Your yeomen are with you and we'll give cover all we can. Out.' Grant waved and spoke into his microphone. The tank's engine puffed exhaust smoke as Brown put his foot down. She nosed into the lane, tracks clawing for a grip until in a rush she burst through and landed with a thump the other side. Simultaneously Partridge manoeuvred so that his turret entered a gap. He spoke to his gunner. 'Co-ax traverse right. On. Now Raikes, give that hedge a good long squirt in front of Sergeant Grant as he advances.'

The Browning gun rattled in rhythmic harmony, dust erupting as the bullets tore the earth and brushwood, tracer bouncing high in exuberance or burning low and sultry in the soil. Grant steered cautiously ahead, inclining slightly to the right. In conformity, the infantry pushed through the hedge and walked warily in his wake. At that moment the orchard to the right erupted from the stupendous American artillery concentration, a fire which, in effect, was somewhat unnerving to the British infantry, though mighty encouraging to Grant behind armour. An American direct hit on his tank's armour was unlikely to do much harm. Nor was he as surprised as the infantry, because he had been expecting the bombardment whereas, to the infantry, it came without warning. They had not been told and, at first, thought it was enemy shelling: it was a shock.

Then Grant's tank struck the mine, heaved and shook with smoke and dust belching from every crevice – both inside and out. She slewed left under the drive of the undamaged track and detonated a second mine beneath the right rear bogey. Grant swept off helmet and headsets and, glancing round the turret, registered McAteer's complex expression, asking the compound question, 'This can't be happening to me? Shouldn't we bail out? Let's bail out? May I please bail out?'

There was no fire.

'All OK down front?' Grant shouted.

'I'm OK,' replied Brown, 'but something's wrong with Armstrong. Hang on.' Then, 'No it's all right. Knocked a bit silly I reckon. Coming round now. What'll we do?'

A battleworthy minefield is a minefield covered by fire. This one was thoroughly battleworthy, as Partridge immediately was made to understand, for the German 75mm anti-tank gun that lay hidden from his view near the crest had bided its time, the layer picking a moment of maximum confusion when attention became fixed upon Grant's stricken tank. Now the German took a fine point of aim, pressing the firing lever, felt the gun heave on recoil, saw the shot's red tracer converge on target with violet electric sparks from its strike against armour. Then he was traversing furiously right, re-aligning his cross wires on the tank whose turret filled a gap in the hedge. He heard the breach close, felt the gun jump and the tap on his arm that signified reloading was complete, and fired once more. Again the tracer streaked towards the target - and again there was the flash and convulsion of a hit.

The first hit upon Grant's tank bored through the glacis plate, decapitated Brown, streaked firily across the turret and ripped the bulkhead before entering the engine behind. Ammunition was set instantly ablaze; it did not need Grant's urgent shout of 'Out - for Christ's sake out,' to start the turret crew shoving for the hatch through which the sergeant was already impulsively forcing his way. Of this the dazed Armstrong, with flames creeping near, knew nothing. Those who escaped from the turret leapt to the ground and only then gave thought to the men in front. They looked round and with horror saw both drivers' hatches firmly shut. Grant turned to climb back aboard but his foot triggered a mine and the pellets scattered among them, incapacitating them all except Benstead. And Benstead, in shock, froze where he lay, not daring to move to the aid of comrades, terrified the enemy would heap fire upon them. With him the act of self-preservation was of the passive sort.

Partridge himself had seen the first flash from the enemy 75 and shrieked an automatic 'Driver reverse'. It saved them, since his driver had as a trained precaution already engaged in reverse, and the tank moved instantly. Thus the next shot, though on target, was just sufficiently angled to be deflected from the top of the turret, its slipstream flinging Partridge's head against the cupola ring. His troop corporal was in better shape, however, and he too had seen the enemy gun's flash. '75 traverse right, steady, ON,' he demanded eagerly of his gunner. Anxiously he studied the blade vain sight moving into line with the dimly observed target. Then, switching from the prescribed fire order to special pleading: 'Harry, there's a bleeding 88 in that lot of bushes by the side of the trees. Fire.'

'Can't see it!' said Harry.

'Fucking well fire,' cried the corporal, 'and don't bloody argue.' The gun loosed off and shovelled up earth to the left of the enemy gun. 'Now go about five yards right and you've got the bastard. Fire.'

This time Harry detected the target. Again the gun lunged on recoil, smoke oozing from its opening breach until the loader rammed home another round, automatically closing the breach. The shell seemed to land precisely where the enemy gun had been. Bits and pieces lifted into the air. 'Target,' the corporal shouted, 'give 'em another for luck.'

When Grant's tank burst into flames the nearby infantry im-

mediately threw themselves out of sight. The leading platoon, already committed to the open, became engulfed in the turmoil. A corporal section leader, running to the right, put his foot on a mine and the scattering pellets wounded him, two members of the section and, fifty feet further behind, neatly penetrated the skull of the platoon officer as he pushed his way up from the lane through the hedge. Below, in the lane, his platoon sergeant saw him fall, took one look at the carnage in front and called to those in sight: 'OK lads. Hold it there. Let's have a shufti before we go on.' At that the rest of the platoon fell flat where it was and began digging holes or, in the majority of cases, dived into the lane and took cover in the hedgerows on either side. Only the sergeant made an attempt to continue the action by studying ways round to the right. The general tendency, therefore, became one of movement sideways instead of forwards so that, deprived of immediate leadership in the forefront of the battle, a local stalemate supervened.

The brave crawled resolutely among the uncharted mines to rescue the injured infantrymen as well as Grant, Benstead and McAteer where they lay beside the burning tank. Then everything became more hazardous when scattered shell fire began to fall. Von Schilling, who had suffered a temporary but extremely frustrating break in communication with his guns, was back in business and trying to make up for lost time in re-establishing the German artillery's presence. Grant's tank burned hotter than ever when its ammunition was reached by the conflagration. The force of internal explosions and exhaustion of oxygen mercifully stunned Armstrong before the flames reached his body. Feeding on explosives, oil and paint, the fire flashed to the engine compartment: its smoke rose and grew denser, but occasionally drifted low to obscure the rescue operation. Like a time bomb the tank approached the moment when its petrol tank might explode.

If survival and rescue predominated among the more resolute men in 'A' Company, the rest of them had more personal problems upon their minds. The second platoon, arriving at the lane shortly after the first had gone to ground, caught the prevailing infection of defeatism. Under cover of heavy foliage while being intimidated by the thump and crunch of the German shells, they followed the example of those who had already failed and sought places of refuge themselves. Some crowded together, a section filtered into the barn; one or two went even further left and found themselves in company with the broken Highlander platoon where it crouched to the left of the barn, and imbibed their sense of frustration. Three were wounded but none were killed. But they felt beaten. Foxton saw them scatter as the shells fell and turned to the third platoon as it waited in reserve. 'Ted,' he shouted to its commander above the bang of the falling shells. 'Take your boys down to the right and push through up the lane.'

He watched them go and saw them enter the lane. The leaders appeared momentarily on the other side. Then a mine went off. Or was it a shell? A minute later more shells fell and he knew it was no good. The call for survival cried aloud in 'A' Company, the incentive to take enemy life was quelled. Inertia pervaded the entire company, transmitted by Clive Foxton to Simcox. In essence, Foxton reported over the radio, his men had been killed or had gone to ground in face of a deep minefield and heavy fire; he saw no hope of reviving the attack until the mines were cleared. It was predictable: Foxton, brave as a lion himself, had only recently taken command although, in any case, he had never been of the keenly competitive kind. At this moment he based his judgement largely upon guesswork that was induced by the claustrophobic effect of the *bocage*. He could not see and, lacking experience, thought not to seek. And Simcox, prone to sympathize with a subordinate's dilemma and rarely given to overriding his company commanders' decisions, was content to accept the report at its face value. 'A' Company, with its strength still almost intact, stopped and melted from view.

The smoke from Grant's burning tank was faintly visible to Corporal Carter as he led his section in the direction of the orchard. Fortunately for his composure its import was denied, otherwise he might have been overbearingly inhibited by fears for his left flank. The bombardment from American guns stopped as suddenly as it had begun, cut off with a sharpness that accentuated still further the feverish sounds of battle in the British sector. For good or evil, thought Carter, the Limeys are in it up to their necks. He turned to check that his own section was following, that the rest of the platoon was moving too, that some of the right flank platoon was in view and that 'their' tank was in sight. Novak was hanging back a bit but the others were keeping pace and the tank was firing busily at nothing in particular. Well, at any rate he could see nothing of an enemy – not that that meant anything. He signalled to the section not to bunch, but himself moved close to Hoffman with the BAR, preferring to be next to the decisive weapon if something should break. The lane was a mere thirty yards distant. He could pick out individual fruit trees beyond, their branches lopped ragged by shells, and even began to notice the carpet of apples lying thick upon the ground, where the explosions had dislodged them, and the dark brown streaks of fresh earth squirted in all directions from the small shell craters. Then, directly ahead, he detected something which was misplaced in the pattern – something that was different because it moved where all else was still – and all at once he picked out a man crouched behind the water trough. 'Hoffman,' he shouted, 'that kraut by the water trough! Get him!' Hoffman had seen the German machine-gunner too and already was aiming from the hip, throwing a long burst until the magazine ran out, replacing the mag and firing again. The others were taking up the theme, firing their rifles from hip and shoulder as the pace of their advance quickened from a walk to a trot and then an impulsive, straggling charge. Return shots whistled close, coming from far within the orchard – but that was all. Hoffman had chopped the machine-gunner and the section was hunting through dugouts cut deep in the bank, throwing down grenades among them, flushing a single wild-eyed individual in field grey who kept yelling 'Me Polsky! Me Polsky!'

They had arrived and suddenly felt good. 'C'mon, let's get the rest,' roared Novak arriving late but moving farther than the others into the orchard. 'They're on the run.'

'Hold it,' snapped Carter. 'This's far as we go. The company

comes through now. We hold here. Clear them dugouts, kick that
guy up the ass backwards and then stand by.'

Novak shrugged, the others jumped into evacuated German
fox holes and set up their weapons. Briggs arrived, running low,
checking they were safe and in position, letting them know that
the rest of the company was coming through. The tank drove in,
moved left to the corner of the orchard and immediately became
a target for a flurry of von Schilling's shell fire. First one landed
with flash, coal-black smoke and bang, then a clump of them,
followed by a pause and next four more detonations randomly
spaced in time. A direct hit against the tank's side armour threw
molten sparks broadcast, like the tapping of a miniature furnace.
The tank shuddered, revved loud, scuttled backwards and
toppled out of sight into the lane. The nearby infantry ducked
low and waited. Briggs ran back whence he came. 'Bet we don't
see him again,' snarled Novak.

But Briggs sought the crisis where it was worst on the
American side – as acute as at Vertefeuille Farm for the British
– to where his Company Commander lay dead from a sniper's
bullet, in a vacuum in leadership and command. At company HQ
fifty yards behind the firing line, he discovered suffocating doubt
and uncertainty. The two uncommitted platoons that were
supposed to have advanced through his own had merely taken
root in the shelter of the orchard's perimeter. From the top of a
knoll he examined the scene and saw tanks hanging back as a
smattering of shellfire made desultory bangs among the trees,
bursting high among the branches and scything the surroundings
with splinters – whether German, American or British it was
impossible to tell. Nobody seemed to be taking a lead, everybody
was lying flat and not a shot was being fired at the enemy. To
Briggs it seemed positively suicidal for the company to remain
where it was. He ran to the nearest tank where it stood, guns
silent and engine ticking over, climbed up from behind and hit
the startled commander smartly on the head. 'What the hell . . .'
came the response.

'Listen,' said Briggs angrily. 'This whole goddam thing's
coming to a stop. My chief's been killed so I'm taking over. Give
me five minutes to get them sonofabitches moving down there

and then d'you reckon you can come into that orchard with us? We'll be safer the other side than here if they step up this goddam shelling.'

The tank commander looked quizzically at Briggs, admired and hated him for his pluck but drew confidence from an outgoing authority. 'You move them, brother,' he said, 'and I'll come too.'

'Kay - see you.'

Briggs jumped to the ground and re-entered the orchard. 'Okay you guys,' he yelled. 'Let's move out. You men with the BAR, shoot one mag each into the trees, the rest come with me.'

Some did not bother to look round, a few displayed mild curiosity and an officer, for whom Briggs had scant liking, actually turned his back. But a BAR man lifted his head and then his weapon, to throw a reluctant burst into the orchard. To the right another took it up, and then there were more and the air was full of lead. Briggs took two steps forward.

'Let's go,' he called.

Shyly men stood up, grasped their weapons, looked sideways to see they were in company and, finding they were, hesitantly walked. Insidiously a wave of renewed confidence and energy caught their interest so that, when the sniper shot once more, he was hazed by a blast of fire which made him abandon the contest. 'C'mon then you bums,' bawled a sergeant and compulsively they surged ahead. Enemy shells burst high and three men fell, but the rest kept advancing from tree to tree, shooting hard at shadows. The racket stimulated their courage and so they fired berserk - becoming, in fact, as much a menace to themselves as the enemy, so much lead did those from behind pump near those in front. But Briggs, moving in the van, enwrapped in the daze of his own achievement, neither had the heart nor the urge to stop them. And when a pair of Germans emerged from cover with their arms raised, it was he who gave the unpremeditated order to fire and execute them. Later he felt utterly ashamed - but the war was a lot older before nightmare visions of that event began to return.

The Americans reached the far edge of the orchard and there sought shelter. By then the air was thick with bullets coming from all directions. There, too, the euphoria evaporated as suddenly as the demand of commonsense self-preservation substituted itself for the previous spontaneous and outright aggression. The tank, which had obediently reacted to Briggs's insistence, came jinking among the trees to take post on the edge of the orchard, its commander scanning keenly for enemy near the tall trees on the crest that were at last in full view.

From the left, above Vertefeuille Farm, the German Jagdpanther, taking its chance amid the British shell bursts, eased into position, its gun grazing the shrub tops of the lane. Unteroffizier Pankewitz fixed his attention on the American tank, which had so fortuitously offered itself, and gave terse orders to his driver who swung left. A curt description of the target's location to the gunner and the 88mm gun was being aimed centrally at its prey. A quick glance round, checking that he remained hidden from view of the enemy near the farm, and then the order to fire. At the vicious crack of the big gun the enemy tank seemed to leap and belch flame. Easy! Pankewitz told his driver to withdraw. The deed was done and undetected, he hoped, by the foe.

16   A Matter of Communication

Simcox and his group of vehicles were parked behind the crest overlooking the battlefield.

'As I understand it we're in one hell of a bugger's muddle,' he announced. ' "C" Company beaten flat on the left, "A" stuck fast on the right – they may have one platoon disengaged but that'll not get through the minefields nor carry far beyond even if it tries.' Turning to Krantsky he added, 'Seems only you Yanks have made much sense so far.'

'You're welcome, Colonel,' said Krantsky with a smile, 'but don't feel too sore. We've troubles too. I've just called Battalion. They've pushed through to the other side of the orchard but there's an 88 or something knocking hell out of our tanks – looks as though it might be from up above your farm over there. The left company lost its commander too. They need time and can't be helped because the rest of the battalion's stalled on the other flank, short of the objective.'

Simcox listened in silence, plunged in thought. Culpepper chipped in. 'Where d'you say that gun is, Bob? How close to the farm?'

'Bit beyond they reckon, maybe firing from behind the crest outa sight of you.'

Culpepper spoke on the radio, questioning his FOOs for sightings of this new threat while Parrott, the Tank Liaison Officer, radioed Snow to give warning of the new danger.

Simcox reflected that his original design had disintegrated into scuffles fought by knots of men acting on local initiatives, men he could not see and over whom he had lost control. That was not unusual but it might take hours to re-establish contact with them and hours were unlikely to be granted. As a primer to his thoughts Dick Tranter called him to the radio to hear a request from the Brigadier for information and then a demand that progress should be speeded up. 'All very well for him,' grumbled Simcox privately to himself. Yet he admitted the justice of the order and stared again at the map, alternating this study with re-examination of the smoke-smudged battlefield – what little he could see of it.

'Dick, tell OC "B" and that flail man I want them,' he called to the Adjutant. 'Freddy,' to the Tank LO, 'give Major Snow the situation as we know it here. Tell him I'm abandoning the attempt to take Vertefeuille Farm though I still want pressure put on there. Tell him I'm going to send "B" Company through on the right, using flails to flush the mines. Say I'll give him more details later. All right?'

'Yes, Colonel,' acknowledged Fred Parrott. 'But have you any idea how long this is going to take? We're getting it hot down there, like sitting ducks. If we don't look out they'll pick us off like coconuts. Can we perhaps pull back a bit?'

'That's the last bloody thing you'll do. No, you tell your OC to stay put. Say I expect him to keep the Hun busy while we get reorganized. As for time,' he mused. 'Well, we'll be lucky if we can get anything moving for at least an hour, I'd say. These things take time. He'll just have to sweat it out.'

Walking to his scout car to speak by radio the LO grimaced. Snow would not be one bit pleased about that. He guessed there would either be a straight back-blast or deliberate misinterpretation of orders. It was to his surprise that the rejoinder was mild.

'Able, Wilco,' said Snow slowly over the air, giving a slight pause, and then, 'Tell footed friends we've perhaps got more of a toehold in the farm than he reckons. Say we'll keep shooting there. Roger so far, over.'

'Roger,' acknowledged Parrott in accordance with the radio procedure which dictated that his OC had more to say.

'Hullo Able,' went on Snow. 'I intend trying to get Call Sign 1 past 2 on the right without waiting for your friends – that is if his local boys will go along and if our transatlantic chums on the right will string along too. Over.'

'Able, Roger, Out,' said Parrott and went to explain Snow's scheme to Simcox while Krantsky and Culpepper listened in.

'Yes,' said Simcox after short contemplation and turning to Krantsky. 'What about your chaps, Bob? Can they string along?'

'Can but ask. Give me a minute or two.' He walked to the telephone.

Garston had arrived and so too had Keith Duncan, the Flail Troop Commander. Each had been listening to the radio conversations and had been able to assemble a rough picture in his mind's eye of how the battle was developing. So, guessing the sort of task Simcox must almost certainly give them, they had warned their subordinates of the task which might soon be in store. The commitment of reserves was standard procedure, the remedial action to a commonplace battlefield rebuff. The difficulty, as ever in war, was in persuading several people with different outlooks to move at once in the same direction at short notice without being able to arrange a joint conference at leisure. So far as the 1st East Hampshires was concerned crash action was always liable to be hazardous under Simcox's leadership: firm though his grasp might be in conference, it slackened when he was compelled to disseminate instructions over the telephone and, particularly, the radio. He had never quite overcome his shyness on the air: Tranter reckoned he feared the microphone might bite him. These idiosyncrasies of mental co-ordination were familiar to Garston, Culpepper and Tranter but quite unbeknown to Krantsky, Snow, Parrott and Duncan. It was Tranter, the good staff officer, who, on these occasions, steered his Colonel through a plan's complexities, checking and rechecking that each item of detail was transmitted to the interested agencies, occasionally interrupting Simcox to remind him of some matter that he had left undisclosed to one or other of the subordinates. Simcox's plan was simple enough: to leapfrog 'B' Company through 'A' and keep 'C' engaged at the farm,

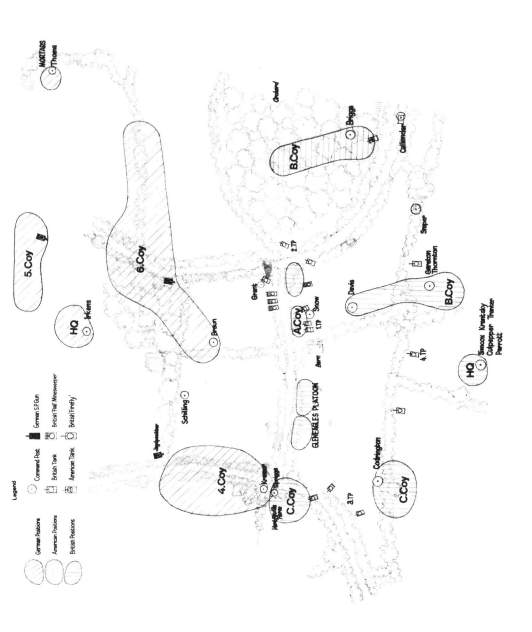

a change from straight left to right swing, to adopt boxing parlance. It needed only minor modification of the original deployment and a mere switching of axis for the reserve company. But Simcox, who preferred to have everything done under his personal supervision, had now to trust to others without having the remotest chance of overseeing their preparations. He was pinned to his headquarters at the centre of a communications network and blinded by the *bocage*.

Timing was crucial – the time it would take the guns, controlled by Culpepper with Pratt's assistance, to readjust to the revised programme; and for Garston to instruct his company, Snow his squadron and Duncan his flail troop. In fact both Garston and Duncan were ready to transmit orders for their new tasks, the former because his platoon commanders had been well briefed by Garston's foresight of such a situation arising, the latter because he, too, had studied the ground and felt capable of positioning his flail tanks accurately under directions by radio without calling his commanders to the sort of ponderous O Group practised by infantry. In this respect – and not fully comprehended by Simcox – the minds of his subordinates raced ahead to implement the basic plan.

Tranter was at full stretch. With one ear he was listening for battle reports from the forward companies, from the tank liaison officer and the gunners for information which would add to his understanding of the situation at the front. With the other he was endeavouring to keep track on Simcox's train of thought and the sequence of orders he was giving. People came and went, the telephone to the Americans was buzzing and Krantsky was not there to answer it: vaguely he remembered seeing the American walk over to talk to Parrott in his scout car. He saw Buttonshaw, the Intelligence Officer, lift the receiver and begin a conversation. He would have to find out about that, but in the meantime David Garston was hastily leaving on the way to briefing his company for the task which would save or lose the battle for them. As was his habit Tranter intercepted Garston in order to verify that they were completely as one in regard to objectives, routes and timings. Garston was impatient to be gone, yet understanding: he, too, knew his Commanding Officer of old and more than once had been saved from error by the Adjutant's vigilance.

Meantime, and without Tranter noticing, Simcox was talking earnestly down the telephone to Robin Callendar who was describing his contribution to the joint plan. The call was corrupted by a somewhat poor connection. Simcox came to understand that the Americans would give fire support from the southern edge of the orchard as the British advance began. Callendar spoke enthusiastically and with pride of his efforts: 'We'll advance on your right once the crest's directly threatened by you British. More than that I'll not promise.' He was wholly honest. Radio communications to his 'B' Company, by SCR 300, were tenuous, and the telephone was as yet unconnected to them. Moreover the company's heavy weapons were still not in position forward. Therefore, it would take an hour or more to restore Baker Company's cohesion when his last remaining reserve was in process of being committed to the right of the orchard where the Germans fought most obstinately.

The telephone conversation ended just as Garston was turning away. Simcox felt a glow of thankfulness towards the American whose integrity had managed to overcome the telephone's distortions. He would not have criticized or made suggestions of amendments even if his mind had worked that way.

'Dick. That was Robin Callendar from the Americans,' he said. 'Just to keep you in the picture, he's putting down some sort of stonk to our right along the crest and then moving some of his boys in behind it when he's ready. OK?'

'Yes, Colonel,' said Tranter, pausing to gather his thoughts while wishing the map was a little closer and wondering where Krantsky was. He must learn more about this! Then Culpepper was talking.

'Colonel, I wonder if you'd let me have a quick check with Dick for a jiffy. This is a trifle urgent.'

A couple of shells landed not far off. They cringed a little.

'Of course, Brian. Help yourself,' said Simcox whose mind was already back with his companies in their predicament.

'Look, Dick,' went on Culpepper, 'we simply must know as near as possible where your leading chaps are or we'll knock hell out of them when things start again. Can I check the locations I've got with your latest gen?'

Reluctantly Tranter turned away to the map and they began a detailed examination of the latest markings. There lurked a half-formed question in his mind, about the American artillery programme because it was imprecise and unconfirmed. But Culpepper's needs were also of vital importance to the East Hampshires. The Americans would have to wait and, in any case, his conversation with the meticulous Culpepper verified his faith in artillerymen of all nations. He let his doubts slide and forgot them altogether as the next phase of the battle unfolded.

Quite unheeded by everybody the clouds had lifted. Where once there had been grey, there were widening patches of blue sky smudged by battlefield smoke. The change was fatally timed. From the north came bombers, squadron upon squadron, heavies and mediums, approaching in tiered swarms, contemptuously ignoring a ragged fusilade from anti-aircraft guns within the German lines. A pathfinder aircraft, lazily circling, dropped red marker flares which shimmered in cascades above the intended target areas. From the leading bombardment formations the bombs were plainly visible as they left the open bays and fell earthward in clusters. Promptly the horizon to the east became capped by rising clouds of smoke and dust where the landscape belched fire like a volcano. More and more bomber waves flew into sight, each guided to a designated target by renewed flurries of carefully aimed marker flares. Vast widening acres were smothered. It was stupendous, the sight of a life-time – for the British and Americans: their attention shifted to this vast out-pouring of fury. They had forgotten it was due.

Yet there was anxiety within the Allied camp. To neither the British nor the Americans was this new. They had seen it at Caen and near St Lo, and each time had been overawed by the immensity of numbers and sound. Only later, after watching bombs miss their target or land short among their own side, had they sceptically come to measure an air attack's military inadequacies in terms of waste and inconvenience. Hence, for almost the total duration of the air attack, nearly everybody tended to stand still. Each combatant soldier focused his attention upon the aircraft's behaviour, warily checking the accuracy of the marker flares and computing the bomb release point for fear there might be a threat to his own safety. Only scattered small-arms fire from places in immediate contention – such as Vertefeuille Farm – fizzled and spluttered like damp squibs in competition with a thunderstorm.

For Garston the bombing interlude served as something more than a fillip to his men's confidence as they braced themselves for assault. While he was being driven at speed to where his subordinates waited, he jotted down notes for the orders he must now give. The bomber attack would keep the enemy quiet, he hoped, and enable him to give his orders uninterrupted. Occasionally he consulted Paul Thornton, who sat in the back of the jeep. It was Garston who dominated. As a junior in a shipping agency before the war, he had been educated to the need for quick, clear thinking. Methods such as those stick. Those under him knew that the simple and precise orders he gave were intended as a monologue. Interjections were forbidden. Instructions flowed in the acknowledged military sequence.

'The position is this,' stated Garston when the O Group was gathered round him. 'The enemy has been cleared from the orchard on the right, by the Americans, and from the hedge to our immediate front – where 'A' Company is now consolidating. But nobody can get on since the tanks have everywhere been stopped by a minefield. On the left it's the same, though 'C' actually have got somebody into the farm where fighting is going on. The enemy have been shelling and mortaring, as you know, and he's produced a self-propelled gun, somewhere near the crest on the left, which is giving trouble to our tanks. Now, the Colonel's intention is to switch the axis of attack from the left to the right and, in conjunction with the Americans, clear the ridge from right to left.'

He paused to let the information sink in and scrutinized his officers, the CSM and Paul Thornton. They wrote notes and drew lines on folded maps.

Garston continued, speaking more quickly because time was short but raising his voice above the bombers' roar. ' "B" Company, gentlemen, will make a gap through the minefield

with a view to seizing the crest line on either side of the lane.
Method. Phase One, a troop of flails, supported by "A"
Squadron of the Yeomanry, will gap the minefield midway
between the orchard and the barn. Four Platoon will move
through the flail gap and form a bridgehead which is to include
the hedge bounding the copse. Phase Two, 5 and 6 Platoons pass
through the gap, in that order, and carry the main assault to the
crest, 5 on the left and 6 on the right.'

Again he paused, behaving like a schoolmaster and double-
checking the lines they drew on their maps to see they conformed
with his intention.

'4 Platoon. Frank,' he said to Davis, 'get your men close under
the hedge, just behind "A" Company, as soon as the flails move
off, and push them through at the double once the flail troop
commander tells you he's successful. He'll be stationed at the
hedge and will give a wave. Clear the objective as thoroughly as
you can and establish a defensive position, paying particular
attention to the front and left flank. I want no interference from
that quarter. Five - Johnny. As soon as Frank leaves the hedge
take his place and then go through the minefield once he is clear.
Then deploy to the right, getting as close to the orchard as you
like because that's clear of enemy. Include the lane in your left
flank and clear it as far as the crest. And watch out for mines. Six
- Bill. Follow up hard, using the lane as centre line but staying
yourself this side so I can find you easily. Fill the gap between
4 and 5 Platoons on the crest and exploit beyond as soon as you
get there. Now, the tanks of the Yeomanry's Number 1 Troop
will be in close support and will pass through the minefield as
soon as they can. Stay clear of them. They draw trouble, as you
know. Two Troop is also, at this moment, trying to filter
through on the right and there'll be American tanks there too.
The gunners are bringing down fire on the crest and I gather the
Americans will also be adding a pennyworth. That's a bonus.
Don't rely on it! Sergeant-major! The section of anti-tank guns
will stay with you and come forward once the objective has been
taken. I'll probably want you to cover our right flank. Details at
the time, though. Medical arrangements as in the original plan.
Communications unchanged. I will move with Company HQ

behind 4 Platoon to take charge in the gap until I am satisfied we are successful in Phase One. After that my entire line will be to the left of the lane. H hour is at 1100 hours.'

He stopped. Checked his notes and looked up.

'Any questions?'

'How about exploitation to the left, sir?' asked Davis.

'Thanks, Frank. The Colonel was not frightfully specific, but I gathered from Dick Tranter that he'll try to pick up "C" Company and shove them up. In any case the rest of the brigade'll probably be moving through after us. But don't get drawn that way yourself. It's thick down there, our chaps are all snarled up in the farm; no one knows where. Just sit tight and deal with anything that comes your way from that direction.'

Again he scrutinized them. Then, 'Well, off you go and good luck. This bombing should have made things easier. Give your section leaders a good briefing. And when the time comes keep them moving.'

'A' Company might have envied their comrades in 'B', if only because they would have had their uncertainties dispelled by a firm lead. But Clive Foxton's stubborn efforts to establish radio contact with his platoon commanders met with only a limited response. One of the platoon sets was 'off net', and so its operator did not hear the messages: another operator could not find his commander: the third, who had heard, could only wait while Foxton kept calling for the others. In the meantime 'A' Company sank out of sight, digging deeper shelters into the hedgerows. To Foxton in this his first action as a company commander, it was a dreadful moment. He had lost touch and, in a mood of appalled frustration, could think of no way of re-establishing it. It simply did not occur to him to go from place to place trying to find the key men and giving that inspiration which they all needed. His mind froze.

In that part of the front, only Snow recognized the air attack as of immediate tactical use. With his tank so positioned that, from the top of his turret, he could get an almost uninterrupted view of the terrain, he thought there was a heaven-sent opportunity to improve his deployment.

'Hullo Tare 3,' he called urgently on the radio as the

preliminary bomber strike fell far away to the left. 'As soon as you can, take advantage of this gefuffle to push a call sign into the outskirts of the farm. You'll never have it easier. Over.'

He had to call twice and McBain's 'Wilco', when at last it came, was far from reassuring in its hesitation. McBain was still recovering from the shock of the panzerfaust, though this Snow was not to know. Next Snow instructed Ingersoll, the Firefly Troop Commander, to support McBain with one of his tanks when the move began. He spoke concisely and persuasively on the air, endeavouring to project his personality through the 'static' crackle of a high-frequency radio channel.

'Hullo 1, Hullo 2,' he called. 'One is to go with their footed friends as already ordered but now's the time to get down the forward slope and join 2 in the lane, just short of the minefield. Meantime, 2, see if you can filter something down the lane, on the right where the Americans seem to be making progress. There's room there by the looks of it, and it may be clear of mines. Over.'

It was then that Snow began to suspect the possibility of hastening Simcox's intention by establishing his tanks in strength on the right flank ahead of the infantry attack.

'Hullo 1,' came Reggie Robertson's reply. 'I'll check with my footman and go if he's fairly happy. Wait. Out.'

'Hullo 2,' said Partridge slowly. 'Very dodgy but I'll try. How about our transatlantic friends? What will they say? Over.'

'Hullo 2. Wait. Out to you,' said Snow and then to Parrott, 'Hullo Tare Able. What about it? Over.'

Parrott had to speak urgently to Krantsky who demurred and then conferred with Callendar on the telephone who had then to ask his tank liaison officer, who had then to check with the American tank company commander, who, too, demurred and then gave tentative approval, warning his tank platoon leaders what might transpire. The approval had to find its way back link by link to Snow, who in turn sent it forward to Partridge, who meantime had braced himself for an advance which, at the outside, would cover two hundred yards and probably less. Robertson, meantime, had dismounted and spoken to Garston who was receptive to any scheme that promised neutralization of the enemy opposed to his own men. But before it was all settled the bomber attack was nearly finished. The benefits of attacking under its cover were almost lost.

Since McBain depended upon the least number of other agencies to carry out his task, he had only to co-ordinate arrangements with his troop sergeant and the designated Firefly commander. That merely required two short radio messages and a couple of words to his driver. To a volley of shots from his supporters McBain's tank burst through the lane, over the hedge and drove full throttle for the farm. Nobody was more grateful than Spriggs to see it arrive, unharmed, in the rubble of the farm's outskirts. Moreover he was somewhat surprised as well. It was an inspiration too. Possibly, he reasoned, it switched the balance in his favour, a balance which, until then, seemed to be swinging the opposite way as some unseen personality on the German side began to make life extremely unpleasant.

Deep in a cellar Kramer, the cause of Spriggs's difficulties, was cursing three terrified fusiliers and chasing them up to ground level to take part in a battle they would much rather have left to others. Indeed Spriggs, of all those in Vertefeuille Farm, was alone in having his head above ground while McBain, with his head below the turret cupola for fear of snipers, watched events only through a single, small periscope. Of those without armour only Spriggs and Kramer had the will to overcome their natural inclinations of self-preservation.

On the opposite flank Robertson and Partridge began to shift their tanks to fresh positions, with Snow conducting their movements to keep them in unison. The Fireflies helped with shots from their 17-pounders directing vicious discharges against either flank. Snow had given consideration to the need for personal leadership but had decided against travelling with his own tank among the two troops as they moved to the right, because to do so would have meant abandoning about the only place from which he could obtain a relatively uninterrupted view of everything in front. The virtues of example, at this moment, took second place to the highly desirable facility of directing the battle from a relatively detached security. This way he could concentrate on dealing with the enemy's reactions while adapting his squadron's activities to the requirements of Simcox's plan. He watched Robertson's tank motor across the field and arrive safely at the lane, where it replaced Partridge's troop which had reversed and turned right to enter the American sector.

Once more, seemingly for the hundredth time, he raised his binoculars and examined the hostile territory, scanning carefully both the crest and the foreground. Quite by chance he happened to be looking at the patch of scrub near the crest above the farm when the long gun slid into view.

In the haze of post-battle analysis Snow was to recall, with amazement, his prolonged reaction to this deadly sight. On the gunnery practice ranges in England he had been among the quickest in barking out fire orders when a canvas target popped suddenly into view. Yet, on this desperate occasion, his mental processes seemed to drop into low gear, proceeding tortuously from decision to decision. Inhibiting questions intruded at every stage. Was it actually happening? Could it really be the enemy? Was nobody else engaging it? Above all, why not one of the Fireflies with their bigger gun? The delay lasted only a few seconds, but it felt an age before he shouted, '75! Traverse left . . .' followed by the drill fire order that brought his own gun into line. Waite, his gunner, never suffered from inertia. Picked for the job on account of his prowess, he instantly recognized the outline of the Jagdpanther and was two seconds settling a point of aim at the centre of that smooth glacis plate (intuitively concurring with Snow's estimate of range at 500 yards). He kicked the firing button, as usual neither feeling nor hearing the gun explode because he was concentrating so intensely upon watching the flight of shot, straining his eyes to detect the tracer streaking red beyond the smoke and dust of discharge. There it was! There, too, a strike – and at the same moment, it seemed, the enemy fired, also across his front – probably at something on the right, obviously not at them. That made it easier. He could pick his next shot, therefore, without fear of enemy counter-fire.

'Got him,' shouted Waite as Snow bawled, 'Target! Go on!!'

The gun jumped as the next round was rammed home. He felt the loader touch his left arm to indicate 'ready', realigned the sight and again hit the button. Dispassionately he registered that the enemy vehicle was reversing, but this time he was not sure whether he had struck home. When lifting debris in the target's vicinity had subsided nothing was left.

Snow was exalted but somewhat deafened by the squeal in his headsets as no less than three excited tank commanders spoke on the air at once, totally jamming the squadron's radio net. When at last it fell silent he first choked them off for poor radio discipline. Then he harried Partridge, telling him to drive for his destination and cover at top speed before the self-propelled gun appeared again, and instructed the Fireflies to keep special watch over the spot where the gun had appeared. Finally he confirmed the enemy presence to Parrott who relayed the information to Simcox, Culpepper and Krantsky.

News of the Jagdpanther reached Garston as, all nose-heavy with their booms down, the flail troop lurched by. He took the opportunity to wave their leader to a halt and warn him of the self-propelled gun's presence. But Duncan already knew since his radio was netted to Snow's from whom he expected - indeed, demanded - close protection once his machines were in full view and committed to their slow, highly vulnerable task of pounding the minefield. Of one thing they were all uncomfortably aware. Bombing or no bombing, the enemy still possessed the will and capability to fight. This would be no pushover. Indeed, Garston, in this interim period between orders and action, began asking himself how the Germans managed it. What was the secret which allowed them to take such fiendish punishment and yet, invariably, come back with fists flying? Loathe them as he did, they had to be granted the full measure of respect.

17 Irkens in Solitude

To Irkens the appearance of the first heavy bomber formations flying in from the north came as no surprise. After instructing Barentz to warn Regimental HQ in addition to his own companies - those, that is, which were still in contact - he moved to a trench outside the farm to watch developments. Better there, he thought, than being trapped in the cellar. The bombs descended upon neighbouring units to the eastward in a reverberating thunder of tremors that bit deep into his stomach. It seemed clear that each successive formation, guided by marker flares, was converging unerringly on the zones where senior headquarters and guns lay thickest. Selfishly he preferred neighbouring units to be struck instead of his own, but that did not moderate his horror of the bombing's significance. Miss him though they might, soon his battalion would be isolated. Yet safe in the knowledge that the first wave on his front was still dropping its load a mile distant, he noted, with studied calm, that the twin-engined bombers passing overhead had US markings. This mental detachment was typical of him in moments of crisis: he rather suspected it derived from his mother's artistic streak, which he deprecated. The next wave added its engine note and bomb whistle to those which had passed, creating a deeply resonant throb, and then there was another wave and yet another, the last dropping its load closer than all the rest, sucking up dust clouds, and momentarily blotting out the sun. This, he reasoned, was the penultimate moment: the next wave would aim for him.

He crouched lower in the trench and fatalistically waited. But the din of engines receded, the thunder of bombing ceased. Only the billowing dust and smoke remained to swell the scene. In disbelief it dawned upon him, as the softer rattle of battle from the north reasserted itself, that they had been spared.

The view from close in rear and farther off to the east was appalling. Trees had vanished or were canted, lop-sided and shredded. Panoramas which had been screened were disclosed by the wholesale demolition of intervening features and thrown into changing reliefs as the smoke and dust eddied and swirled. He ran to the cellar. Down there they were outwardly calm, shaking off dust. The atmosphere seemed more fetid than ever from the sweat of men in terror. Barentz was firing questions into a telephone. The rest of the staff, so far as he could see, were calm, though pale, at their posts, listening to Barentz. He, too, waited for Barentz to finish speaking, impassively studying the Leutnant's face as the conversation proceeded, noting the inflections upon each short acknowledgement of information received, narrowing his eyes at the ultimate question from his subordinate. 'Is there anything at all you can do?'

'That was the Gunner – von Schilling,' said Barentz to Irkens as he replaced the handpiece.

'Report,' he demanded.

Barentz glanced at his map, gathered his thoughts, and chanted in the manner he reserved for moments of crisis. 'The enemy presses hard along the entire divisional front but there is only fragmentary information from the right where infantry and tanks have advanced, in places, up to 2,000 metres. There is no contact with either Regiment or Division or the other battalions. No contact either with 4th Company at *Graben*. We know the enemy have penetrated most deeply on their right and in the farm outbuildings on their left with infantry – though, there, tanks have been repulsed. On the left Sixth Company has been under heavy fire, many British and American tanks and men are building up to the front and round the left flank. Leutnant Weber is very worried and calls for more artillery fire. As for Fifth Company – well, they are intact and, like ourselves, have escaped the bombing. All mortars, too, are in action though

ammunition supplies are fast running low.'

'I see,' said Irkens. 'So, though it is on the right where we are most in peril, it is on the left where the enemy throws his strength. What is the artillery state?'

'No contact with artillery area, sir, since the bombing, but von Schilling is still in touch with us.' He spoke the aristocratic name with that tone of disdain which, as a Bavarian, he was accustomed to apply to Prussians.

'Call him,' demanded Irkens. A moment later the call was connected.

'I have no contact with my guns,' reported von Schilling, 'but we are doing all we can to re-establish both by radio and line. The enemy to our front seems quiet by the farm but, on the left, both the British and Americans are building up near the orchard. Something big is coming from there. There has been shooting between our Jagdpanther and their tanks.'

Irkens looked hard at the map, pondered deeply and spoke again to von Schilling.

'I too am trying to regain contact with the gun area but if you get through first say that I intend to launch 5th Company in counter-attack once the enemy gain a foothold within the *Seydlitz* position on the left. The pre-planned fire tasks will be employed unless otherwise ordered. In the meantime keep me informed of the situation at Vertefeuille Farm. Report, too, when you are speaking to your guns again.'

Turning to Barentz he went on, 'Very well, you heard that. Tell Company Five and then instruct the mortars to concentrate their fire against anything moving on the left flank.'

He returned to further contemplation of the map, taking cursory notice of Hauser on the telephone: the man looked paler than usual but they were all a little overwrought. Baumler, his servant, pushed a mug of warm coffee into his hand. He smiled in gratitude. They had been together for two years and each understood the other's requirements in time of crisis, appreciating, above all, that speech must be reduced to the minimum. But Baumler had something to say on this occasion and indicated to Irkens it must be in confidence. They moved aside.

'What is it, Baumler?'

'It's Hauser, Major. He's out of sorts. Like Kessel that time at Smolensk. I know the signs.'

Irkens looked over to where Hauser was manning the telephone and recognized a sort of listlessness. 'Thanks, Baumler,' he said. 'I'll keep an eye. Are you all right?'

'I'll do,' said the soldier. 'We've been in tighter spots before. You never let us down then.'

Irkens was touched but grateful for Baumler's expression, coming as it did from the one man present who was allowed to take such a liberty. For Irkens mostly maintained a discreetly distant relationship with his battalion, even with those who stood closest at headquarters. As a result he was lonelier than the average commander though more careful than a great many in keeping touch with the lower ranks. His was a studied attitude, acquired from experience, yet one which suited his gentler Swabian temperament.

Hauser was talking to Company Five on the telephone, his voice abrupt, underlining the meaning of Baumler's suspicions. The company was reporting its readiness for counter-attack. 'What,' Irkens asked himself, 'were their chances of success if they had to execute his order?' It had been formulated as a last resort. To commit one's only reserve in order to re-establish an already lost position represented desperation. Ideally the counter-attack should be made at greater than company strength, preferably by a complete reserve battalion. That was impossible here - even if, as was unlikely, the designated units were intact and unharmed by the bombing. Irkens had adjusted his plans to satisfy the worst possible case. Help from outside was no longer to be expected. He was compelled to fall back upon his own resources - and even these were severely deprived so long as contact with the artillery was broken. He considered asking again whether or not the gunners were now in touch, but resisted the temptation. That might disclose a premature anxiety. The principal basic requirement of the moment was a demonstration of mutual confidence - or at least some sort of belief in the outcome. One retrograde step, one sign of weakness, one hesitation, and the whole bunch might take flight.

He gave detailed consideration to Company Five's forthcoming task. By a single predetermined order he had begun what was, after all, a routine automatic process. The Company Commander knew his role because, together, they and the principal subordinates had twice rehearsed it in days gone by. Yet the daily toll of casualties had so diminished manpower that the infantry's capacity to hold the objective was doubtful. It was now questionable whether they could reach their objective at all because the prime elements of fire support that were so necessary to shake the enemy - the artillery, mortars and assault guns - had suffered so severely that the plan's original foundation was undermined. Was he right to persevere? He asked Barentz for a report on the latest assault gun state. That at least was reassuring. Half an hour ago they were in running order, and though the Jagdpanther had just been damaged it was fit for action again and had shifted behind the crest in the hope of baffling the enemy gunners when next it engaged from a different place.

To the east the battle roared louder and – somewhat disturbingly – seemed to be wheeling fast to the south, curling in
waves of sound round the right flank in confirmation of
Barentz's report that the enemy had penetrated to some depth.
On the face of it, that was where the main enemy effort was
being made. It occurred to him that, though the enemy artillery
bombardment had been heavy on his front initially, its scale had
been light by comparison with what was frequently employed by
the British or Americans in major assaults. Also that the attacks
had been tentative and not pressed with great determination. He
wrestled with a notion that the enemy rated his sector as of
minor importance, perhaps to be by-passed, and that, within an
hour or so, he might be encircled by an opponent who was
demanding his surrender.

18 Callendar Rubbernecking

Lieutenant-Colonel Robin Callendar could be accused of many failings - as he would have been the last to admit - but inflexibility was not one of them. It was true that he had been prejudiced against co-operation with the British in the first place, but Simcox, by his straightforwardness, had overcome this feeling and so far he had no reason to regret his change of heart. Simcox was keeping to the bargain too: the fact that there was partial failure was hardly his fault - or so it seemed from Bob Krantsky's reports. But Callendar was under pressure from a senior commander just as Simcox was under pressure from his Brigadier. This led him to a bout of self-criticism: by not throwing greater weight against his left flank instead of the right, he had failed in fact wholly to support the British. He had just temporized and in doing so wasted the opportunity. For the thrust by 'B' Company had made much better progress than the rest of the battalion put together and there could be no doubt that the British activity had largely contributed to this. He could kick himself. Now, with his reserve committed to the right, he lacked sufficient resources to exploit an apparent success on the left. One thing alone he could do to redeem matters. Although he could not inject fresh manpower he could, at least, boost fire support. In addition he could assert his personal influence by taking the lead at the front. When Callendar told Simcox he would provide 'the works', he meant the fire of every gun, mortar and tank he could command.

'Give me everything you've got,' he demanded of his staff as they leant over the map, 'and give it quick – here, here and here.'

His index finger pushed into the map. At the third stab it marked the extreme flank position and overlapped by half a knuckle into the British sector. Major Aron Potter, the Operations Officer and the Artillery Liaison Officer looked dubious, but on their maps marked circles exactly where Callendar's finger had rested.

'Don't argue. Do it,' he commanded, 'and do it to this schedule.' He slapped down on the table a list of timings he had scrawled before speaking to Simcox. 'OK! I'm rubbernecking and I'll be there on the left when those guns start firing. Don't forget it's to help the Brits as much as us so they make our job easier. Lay that shoot on thick so it makes their hair curl.'

The artillery officer picked up his telephone and the orders began to flow to the staff at the gun command post a mile in rear. Callendar took his carbine and made for his jeep. He read anxiety on Potter's face.

'You aren't going to leave me to it?' Potter asked. 'All hell's likely to pop soon and you may be needed here, sir. What if Colonel Blower comes down?'

'Tell him I've done what he always said we should do when the chips are down – gone to lead from the front and not from the ass! No, don't worry, Aron, about him or me or anything except keeping people moving the way you know they're meant to go. I'll back you and in the last resort there's the radio.' More comfortingly he added: 'I figure that Baker Company might need a toe up the ass, specially now they've no commander. There's going to be problems with the Brits coming through there and I reckon somebody'll have to be around to see we don't get Bunker Hill in reverse. All you've got to see is that the cannon fire gets started on time and gives the Brits no chance to complain.'

He arrived on the northern edge of the orchard as the first rounds of the renewed British bombardment were beginning to strike the crest. Parked alongside the thick hedgerow he found two of his own 57mm anti-tank guns, their crews lying low in the lane.

'What are your orders, Sergeant?' he demanded of the

detachment commander.

'To join Company "B" on their objective, sir.'

'Why aren't you complying?'

'Can't get through, sir,' replied the NCO uncomfortably. 'There's all hell up there. Nothing can get through.'

'All hell my ass,' replied Callendar. 'That's mostly our stuff, Sergeant. If I can go there you can too. Get those guns moving and let me see you there pronto. Follow me through that gate.'

Argument he felt would be unnecessary judging by the sergeant's expression. The order would be obeyed, as confirmed by the NCO's urgent shouts at his men. Callendar drove fast through the gate among the shattered trees and at once came upon men from Company 'B' digging foxholes. These were Briggs's platoon, commanded now by a sergeant. Here too he found immobility except from litter-bearers plodding through the trees carrying the company's wounded. One of the men waved cheerily from his litter. 'State side and a Purple Heart for me, Colonel,' he called. 'You'll be back,' riposted Callendar and sought out the platoon sergeant, asking the same question he had put to the anti-tank detachment commander.

'What are your orders, Sergeant Pollack?'

'None, sir, 'cept stay here,' said the Sergeant, adding, 'Lieutenant Briggs took the rest of the company on through the trees and left his outfit here. We ain't heard nothing since then.'

'What's your state?' asked Callendar.

'We're OK, sir. Got here without much trouble 'cept for that goddam sniper, who gotten the Captain and two or three guys clipped by mortars.'

'Fine. Well, take your platoon forward to your company's right. Stop this side of the orchard boundary and stand by to advance on further orders. Clear?'

'Yes, sir. Let me get them off their asses and they'll be there. Will you tell the Lieutenant?'

Callendar agreed and continued his progress deeper into the orchard, searching for Briggs. He had transgressed military propriety by interfering in a subordinate's command. He had also risked adding confusion to an already involved situation. He noticed Sherman tanks slowly entering the orchard behind him.

Somehow they looked kind of different from the US sort. Then he grasped that these were the British - had he but known it, Partridge's. He recalled hearing something from Krantsky about this. This orchard was getting mighty crowded and he dreaded what might happen if the Germans decided to repeat their earlier bombardment of its interior. At this very moment, too, he guessed, the reserve British company would also be approaching the area, crossing the field to the left or even edging into the orchard. Callendar shut his mind to the dangers and quickened his pace, seeking an opening in the branches that shrouded the orchard's periphery. Here he found Briggs and began to explain the plan of action.

Briggs listened intently to his Colonel's scheme - hearing of the intensive and heavy bombardment which was going to blast the enemy to their front just when the British were rising to the assault; the intended, impromptu redeployment of his own platoon closer to the crest in readiness for exploitation once the British were seen to be making progress. All this he grasped with gratitude from a commander who had arrived, full of ideas, at the moment his own initiative seemed to have run dry. To take umbrage at his authority being usurped did not occur to him - that sort of behaviour, he might later discover, was reserved for hindsight by senior commanders. To him, in the moment of crisis, every scrap of advice and aid was priceless. Quite unnervingly he had found himself, within a matter of minutes, at the head of a company instead of a platoon, confronted by a foreign situation that was almost out of control. Here he was, on the company's final objective, and not at all sure what to do next. The workings of a company were unfamiliar to him. Throughout training he had tended to concentrate every effort upon running his platoon to the exclusion of what went on around it. The platoon he had learnt to handle instinctively, but each move of a company, he now suddenly discovered, had to be carefully thought out with foresight as to the unimaginable in the heat and noise of battle. Allied to fear and fatigue his mental processes cloyed. A reduction in the intensity of demand for immediate action blunted his determination.

In a momentary lull in the gun fire, as the British gunners

lifted their sights from one target to the next, a new sound reached Briggs's ears - and intrigued his Colonel too. From somewhere to the left and rear came the roar of tank engines followed by a furious clanking as of somebody throwing gravel against a tin fence. There was, too, the crack of high-velocity guns firing to their flank and, occasionally, random explosions like mines detonating. The noises came from what they assumed to be friendly territory, yet its unfamiliar tone bred apprehension. The sight of a soldier running towards them through the trees made them fear the worst.

'Lieutenant,' he said excitedly, 'there's the strangest goddam thing down there you ever seen. A sort of tank but with chains whirling like a dancer's fan in front and kicking up one helluva ruckas.'

Braun heard it, too, and peered timorously to his front, fearing some incomprehensible manifestation of war - perhaps the sort of secret weapon which propaganda suggested was the sole prerogative of German inventors. But nothing was to be seen through the dense hedgerows except a smudge of thickening dust and flying dirt that arose to mix with the smoke-laden atmosphere. He looked sidelong at his companions and shrugged his shoulders. Time would tell. For the moment they must stay where they were, if only because a move in any direction was far too perilous to contemplate. There was battle to front and flanks and the thunder of bombardment behind. Resignedly Braun began to debate ways to terminate his contract with battle. Cut off as he was from his officers and senior NCOs, the negotiation of surrender might be simplified. Conscience, allied to military duty, seemed gradually to atrophy as fear lodged deeper in his belly.

19 The Minefield

That people should regard his strange-looking machines with astonishment was nothing new to Keith Duncan, the Flail Troop Commander. His Sherman tanks, each with a protruding boom that carried a rotating flail drum, were oddities which some called 'Funnies', partly from the impression they gave when the drum and chains whirled and beat the ground into a whirlwind of mud and dirt. Duncan's immediate concern, however, was not directed towards technical wonderment but the tedious and yet vital problem of accurate *bocage* navigation. He personally led the other three flails to within a field's length of the point where they were to start flailing, and supervised their exact alignment to the axis of advance. Now he waved them on. Led by the sergeant's vehicle, they were overlapped in echelon so as to create a minefree path, three flails wide, through the crust of the enemy position. With crisp, radioed directions he guided them to the point in the lane where the 'gapping' operation was to begin.

The sergeant's tank halted five yards short of the lane and the others took station to its rear. Duncan watched them jerk as rotors were engaged in drive to the main engines, and saw each tank's turret traverse to the side, steering its gun clear of mine explosions when they occurred. He glanced right and left to reassure himself that the supporting Pentland Yeomanry tanks were in position and ready to give support. This was crucial for, when in full operation, the flail tank crews were blinded by debris and quite unable to engage the enemy themselves. A second exploratory glance and then he spoke again on the air: 'Hullo Dog to Able. Well done. Start flogging. Out.'

The flail tanks engaged gear, revved, spun their rotor drums and began a convulsive advance. Simultaneously the tanks of Pentland Yeomanry thrust their guns through the hedges, challenging any machine or man who might be tempted to interfere. Even a few members of 'A' Company, low in hedgerows and long grass, inquisitively raised their heads, and one in the front row, just to the right of the flail path, actually began firing his Bren gun in the general direction of the enemy, contributing a tentative solo effort to this fresh initiative.

David Garston raised an arm to Frank Davis as the signal for his platoon to advance, saw Davis stand up and watched them file through the hedge and disappear from view in the direction of the selected start line where the flails were churning. At that he too stood up, followed by his companions of Company HQ and walked towards the start line. Already Davis's platoon was deployed. Each section advanced in file to facilitate its passage through gaps in the next hedgerow, the men moving slowly but calmly in immaculate formation: each man privy to his own special dread – fear of death, of mutilation, of his own frailty of moral fibre; perhaps, worst of all, suffering from anticipation of the unknown – some happening for which his training had left him unprepared or which his imagination could never encompass. Happy, indeed, were those without imagination who walked forward, as did Corporal Parker, with a mind that worked in blinkers, concerned only with immediate surroundings and the specific task of keeping his section under control. There were others who saw things more sharply outlined.

Garston was in time to witness the hedge erupting into shreds at the pummelling from the flail. Fascinated he saw the minesweeper cut through bank and branches, followed by its companions which widened the hole. In the intensity of concentration he barely heard the crack of supporting tank guns as they fired speculatively at points in the *bocage* where the enemy might be hiding. The flails were a centre of attraction – and for retaliation. All at once a dialogue of explosions began, German mortar bombs descending in a cluster in front of the hedge near Grant's blazing tank, and in close proximity to the flails. Simultaneously flame and smoke leapt from beneath the leading flail's rotor, the boom jerked up, a chain soared in a lazy parabola from its detonation of a mine – and the boom dropped back to the horizontal. Garston saw Davis's platoon pause, the men kneel and lie down at the subaltern's order. From close by he heard Paul Thornton, the gunner OP, speak into his radio.

'I'm trying to get something onto those bloody mortars, David,' he called. Garston waved an acknowledgement, well knowing how unlikely it was that anything would be achieved since the precise location of the mortar positions behind the distant trees and crest was almost impossible to ascertain. Nevertheless the mortar fire subsided and Garston was relieved to see Davis stand up, shout at his men, and one by one, platoon sergeant, section leaders and then the whole bunch, rise to their feet and start forward again, making hurriedly for those gaps in the hedge that were adjacent to the flail path. Perhaps, thought Garston, they were a little ahead of schedule. They were intended to reach the hedge at about the moment the flails, advancing at their ludicrous $1\frac{1}{2}$ miles per hour, were ending their task. That way there need be no loss of momentum: the platoon could keep moving, running by sections through the flail path, to redeploy wide on the other side and establish the bridgehead through which the remainder of the company must advance. But the flails were still pounding because, periodically, mines were being detonated. Moreover – yes, one flail had shuddered, was stopped and burning, its crew members struggling from the hatches, hopping across the engine deck and running down the path they had just opened.

Neither Duncan nor anybody else had seen the Jagdpanther fire its fatal shot at the flail because Pankewitz had been extraordinarily careful to conceal his approach and had reversed out of sight within seconds of firing. But his local victory sharpened the watchfulness of his opponents. It was Ingersoll in his Firefly who, a moment later, caught a glimpse of the German vehicle's hull through shrubbery, traversed his gunner on target, gave a succinct description of its location and observed the 17-pound solid shot strike home. Though it failed to penetrate

the main armour Pankewitz sensed at once the finality of the hit.
The crown of the driving sprocket was severed, depriving the
track of power. Because the Jagdpanther was thus immobilized it
was also, for all practical purposes, reduced to impotence in a
location which, though concealed by shrubbery from view, was
unprotected from fire. Lacking motive power its gun's traverse
was limited to 8° either side of centre to the front only. The
enemy had merely to fire in its general direction and eventually
the vehicle would be reduced to scrap metal. Next moment a shot
ripped through the side armour smashing the engine. Something
passed overhead with a violent 'crack' and earth flew high to the
front. The others in the crew were looking at him hard, all asking
the same unspoken questions. He could hear fluid gushing into
the engine compartment. The reek of fuel reached his nostrils.
'All right. Get out of here,' he commanded and pushed back the
hatch, heaving himself aloft and flinging himself to the grass
followed by the others. Again the Jagdpanther was hit in flank as
they picked themselves up and ran fifty yards. Behind there was
a rending crunch at the culminating penetration and the ammunition in their vehicle exploding.

Garston was aware of the flurry of tracer whipping into the
bushes where the Jagdpanther lay and guessed their purpose, but
his attention was mainly focused on the flail lane, worried that

the loss of a flail would block it. But the two surviving flails went their ponderous, clanking way, seemingly oblivious of their comrades' fate. Moreover the detonation of mines was at an end: for ten yards they flailed without again striking one. Duncan bawled down the radio: 'Hullo Dog to Able and Baker. OK. Stop flogging, stop flogging and wheel clear, over.' They acknowledged by disengaging flail drive, trundling away to right and left of the lane amid some shallow dips in the ground, traversing their guns to the front and joining in the universal peppering of the tree line with high-explosive and machine-gun fire. Garston impatiently waited for Davis and his men to start, dreading that something might prevent them, angry that there should be even the slightest pause, yet sympathizing with the platoon commander who was faced with one of the most difficult feats in battlefield leadership – re-energizing a platoon in face of a belligerent enemy.

Yet, when Davis rose to urge his men on, they responded, albeit more slowly and with greater reluctance than before, because now, although they were partly hidden from sight, they were entering the acknowledged beaten zone of the enemy defensive fire. Davis led the first section in person, passing Grant's tank in flames on the right and then the burning flail to the left. Fanned by the heat from them both, he neither looked right nor left at the wrecks but steadily ahead. He stopped at the exit and unobtrusively beckoned his followers to move towards the trees on the crest. From somewhere behind he became aware of dreadful screams but shut his ears, preferring not to guess what agony caused them.

The next section was approaching, led at the trot by the stolid Parker, Sten gun in hand. His Bren gunner and Number 2 were in close attendance, followed by the riflemen with set faces. As they went by he roared at Parker, 'Left sector, Corporal Parker, and keep a bloody sharp eye on the farm. God knows who's there – us or them – but that's the place to watch for.'

Parker replied, 'Sir', in his parade ground voice, and ran on. Davis scrutinized them keenly and was shocked at Cain's visage. A face of self-assurance had turned into a distorted mask of incredulity. Yet there had been no such sign before they set forth, no warning of change. Why? Or was he imagining something?

Cain had pressed through the hedge and entered the flail path uplifted by his usual self-confidence. He saw some tank men, one yellowed with shock and moaning; another staring, sightlessly; and a third applying a dressing to the torn stump of the first man's leg. Those were the survivors from Grant's crew. Slightly to the right of the muddied, beaten flail path he got his first close look at death in its contorted form – not the tidy image that newspapers and cinema occasionally presented, but a twisted and heaped bundle of flesh, blood and bones thrown into disorder and blackened by close contact with high-explosive. The sight fascinated and yet repelled him. He tried to tear his eyes away and instead became engrossed by the horror. Something warned him that, at any moment, he might be reduced to the same mess. A few yards further on stood the burning flail, flames leaping through the turret hatch, smoke belching from the engine compartment, bursting ammunition rapping its interior. From inside, without prelude, he heard the incoherent, rending screams (which Davis had heard and as instantly had shut from his mind) – the cries of a man in utter desperation, roasted by flames, tearing blindly with scorched and blistered hands at a jammed hatch lever in a final frenzied delirium of consciousness before the flames and smoke choked him. They all registered it but none clearer or with more penetrating insight than Cain who at once felt joined in spirit and experience with that man in torment. The screams lasted for as long as it took Cain to trot fifteen yards – awful seconds in which his whole outlook changed. He left the minefield in a daze, busily converting his purple dreams of war into a nightmare of black reality.

Blindly Cain followed Trefall who, in turn, followed the Bren group who followed Parker. The tree line ahead was a misty green in which nothing moved. Yet the effects of the burst of fire from Braun's machine-gun which cut Trefall in half was luridly distinct. Cain seemed to see it in slow motion as the shattered man jack-knifed. All constraint abandoned him. He turned about and ran down the slope, racing for the gap in the minefield where Davis saw him coming. Avoiding the officer he veered into the ground untouched by the flails. The inevitable happened. He stepped upon a mine and was flung down. At once the panic was dispelled. As suddenly as it had gripped him it was replaced by an awful clarity of vision, the concept that he was caught in the open and sentenced to die. Two yards to the left he could see the beaten turf of the flail path that represented safety. He tried to stand but rose only to his knees before a paralysing weakness withdrew every ounce of strength from his legs. Again he collapsed and struggled to rise, meanwhile hearing somebody screaming, and wondering who else was in such dreadful straits until he realized that the screams came from himself. He had discounted the yarns of fiction which told of people in distress hearing their own screams with detachment. The realization that he was victim of the same hallucination in some way concentrated his mind upon his danger. It made him realize, too, that he wanted to live but that rescue might be delayed. Nobody in the platoon or the rest of the company would have time for him. He would suffer.

None of this had been visible to Garston who, with Thornton, was approaching the minefield after signalling to the rest of the company to follow, platoon by platoon, according to plan. At the hedge it was comforting to examine the ground to his front and find no sign of Davis's platoon. That implied they had been successful - or at least had arrived somewhere in the vicinity of their objective. The two surviving flails were still firing and their troop officer had driven up to the lane and, with his machine-gun, was raking the tree-tops ahead. Also Garston thought that he could see yet another tank crawling along the right flank, possibly encroaching upon the American sector. Apart from these the battlefield was inscrutable except, that is, for its sounds and its smells, the odours of explosives, petrol fumes and putrefaction. Gunfire to the right and small-arms fire to the front were interspersed by the thud of exploding grenades - the evidence of a grapple and confirmation of Davis's charge to close quarters. Garston saw, for the first time, that the slope was convex and, therefore, from its base, he could see only the upper parts of the trees on the crest and not where Davis and his men were tackling the enemy. He was gratified to find his second platoon arriving in company with the first of Robertson's tanks. They entered the minefield together and, without hesitation, began climbing the slope. At that moment a clutch of mortar bombs came down with sighs, rending crumps and bursting smoke. The tank kept going – accelerating under its commander's urging. Some of the infantry section fell, two or three ran forward and threw themselves down. A couple raced to the rear.

At the sight of the terrified men tearing towards them the next section wavered and stopped. At once it was obvious to Garston that panic from the running men might be transmitted to the entire company, leaving Davis's platoon in isolation near the objective. He ran to bar their way, arms waving, and clutched a wide-eyed man by the shoulder shouting, 'Come on, it's never so bad once you're in.' The man looked at him in blank astonishment and took an involuntary step forward. Then the rest followed, and the advance continued. Garston stayed with them, calling them on, standing boldly in the centre of the flail path until the entire platoon was complete on the other side of the minefield and he had pointed the way, right inclined, to the platoon commander. All this time more bombs were pitching down, though with nothing like the previous intensity and, fortunately, slightly to the left, hitting only two men. Calmly he then returned to the hedge to supervise the deployment of the third platoon. So instantaneous had been the arrival of crisis and so instinctive his reaction to it that the magnitude of Garston's courage did not occur to him.

The fall of mortar bombs actually guided Garston's choice of his company's axis. The enemy fire, though reduced in volume, was tending to fall more to the left. Therefore he decided to skirt to the right even if this meant an incursion into the American sector. He spoke about this to the reserve platoon commander and accompanied him through the gap until they were a good fifty yards beyond the minefield, with the crest line just coming into sight above the convex slope. The mortaring of the minefield had ceased. There was, he considered, an ominous silence on the part of the enemy heavy weapons, though brisk small-arms fire was chattering among the trees, abetted on the right by longer bursts of belt-fed machine-guns from the tanks.

There was nothing much more that Garston could do at this stage. All his platoons were committed to specific tasks and, except for a group of running khaki figures he observed near the orchard on the right, had disappeared from his view. These, he guessed, were his and not American even though they were within the American boundary. For ten minutes the battle rattled low in infantry key.

The artillery took over again and with a fury that excelled anything so far contributed in this battle, seeming to carpet the crest line to the right and with lesser concentration to the centre and left. It badly shook Garston, for this could only presage the German counter-attack with a timing and strength that were totally unexpected. He devoutly hoped Thornton·was ready to drop a counter-barrage on the far side of the crest, curtaining the objective from an oncoming German assault force. He feared most for the men he had diverted to the right, realizing that they must surely be receiving the brunt of this bombardment before they had time to take all their objectives and become established in readiness to repel the enemy. It was all too obvious, in fact, that the enemy had timed his counter-blow to perfection.

Then it dimly occurred to Garston that there was something odd about the enormous barrage. It looked as if it were arriving from the north and not from the enemy to the south. Step by step his mind assembled a concept of what might be happening until he drew the conclusion that the British gunners had got it wrong and were shelling short – not unprecedented even from the best gunner units. In that case they were shelling too far right and into the American sector as well. Then it occurred to him that the shelling could only be from the Americans themselves – something he certainly had not been warned to expect. Had it been so he would never have dispatched his men so far to the right. A ghastly sensation of futile anger swept him. There was simply nothing he could do to stop .the holocaust which threatened the destruction of his company at the very moment when it seemed poised for success. He cursed every American born – and sprinted back to his radio operator in an attempt to send a message to Battalion HQ in a despairing effort to stem the carnage.

In fact battalion was made aware of the disaster almost as soon as it began. Snow had deduced what was wrong and radioed a warning to Parrott who had, perforce, to run twenty yards to Tranter who at once denied knowledge of any such impending act on the American part. For Tranter was still ignorant of the Callendar-Simcox interpretation of 'the whole works' – or even of any major American artillery intervention at all. So, too, was Krantsky when he was drawn into the conversation, and even Simcox seemed surprised when it was put to him. They became engaged in heated recrimination, arriving at the general conclusion that this must be German fire after all – a solemn warning of the impending counter-attack which Culpepper was ready to meet with a defensive barrage of his own well beyond the crest. They were stiffened in this opinion by the knowledge that a proportion of the fire was falling outside the American boundaries. Therefore, they reasoned, even if the Americans were firing to their own front, they most certainly would not engage targets in the British sector at this stage when British infantry were fully committed to an advance.

Tired minds that were ill-supplied with information, in circumstances of tension and fear, toyed with guesswork. In the dense *bocage* a wide-ranging view of the situation was as impossible to achieve as a cool assessment of the conditions – conditions which, at every turn, were bent by the enemy who, they assumed, would do all in his power to defeat them with the unexpected. But at that moment the Germans, too, were somewhat baffled – as Irkens, trying desperately to discover the extent to which the enemy had penetrated his positions, would have been the first to admit. Yet the one man of senior rank who happened to be closest to the mystery and who might have had the power to stop it in time was himself seriously embarrassed by communication problems of his own.

20   Out of Confusion

To appreciate fully a tragedy one has to have insight into its cause. Lieutenant-Colonel Robin Callendar of the 301st Infantry had watched the British advance and had been cheered by their implacable progress towards the enemy, despite the mortar fire heaped upon them. He had seen that first platoon charge to the tree line, noticed one or two men fall and then had lost sight of them. A little later he observed fresh British infantry moving close alongside the American flank, escorted by their tanks, which were firing briskly into the hedges that screened the crest. Suddenly he remembered his fingers on the map and realized that the artillery fire he had arranged in support of the British – what he had proudly termed 'the whole works' – was liable to fall just where the British infantry was setting foot. And there was absolutely nothing he could do to prevent it; that was for sure, even if his radio set had been close to hand instead of in the jeep which was parked farther back in the orchard. Indeed, with a purr, a whoop and a roar, the first salvo was overhead and bursting deep among the trees and across the intervening meadow. Hypnotized, he watched infantrymen run – neither backwards nor to the flanks, but straight ahead into the heart of the fire, swallowed within a matter of seconds by smoke and dust swirling from the undergrowth.

Callendar turned and dashed full tilt through the apple trees, searching for his jeep, blindly taking the risk that his own men, seeing him run, might copy his example and begin a spontaneous retrograde movement. His single-minded purpose was to reach his SCR 300 radio set and get that disastrous bombardment stopped. Panting, with hands trembling, he grasped the microphone and three times called 'Hullo Item Six for Item Five. For God's sake stop those guns firing. They're dropping on friendly forces. Item Six to Item Five, Over.' Three times there was no reply. Only then did he notice that the aerial antenna had either been snapped by striking a tree or shot away and that, therefore, the signal was not being transmitted. Helped by the jeep driver he rummaged furiously beneath a jumble of kit clogging the back seats and at last found the spares. It was a matter of seconds to replace the rod but then, in clumsy anxiety, he forgot to listen carefully for traffic on the net, spoke without waiting and jammed a transmission already taking place. As a result the listeners at his headquarters control set heard only the end of the message and therefore had to ask for a repeat. And having received the repeat they felt compelled to ask Callendar which serial of the artillery programme he meant. In one wild second Callendar's temper exploded. He bawled, 'Item Six. For Christ's sake listen out . . .' then realized the enormity of his error, said 'Hold on' and fumbled with his pad to identify the correct serial and transmit it as calmly as his disturbed emotions allowed.

When at last Callendar was satisfied that his intentions were understood and ensured that those at the battalion command post would explain to Krantsky what had happened, he returned to look for Briggs again. He found the Lieutenant staring in awe towards the artillery barrage which, of course, could not be stopped at call.

'Did I see men walk into that, sir?' Briggs asked in astonishment.

'You sure did, but forget it. That gunfire's gonna stop and when it does I want you to move to your front and take post on that ridge. You may find some British left. Maybe even a few krauts: but get there and stay there, Briggs, and I'll get what help to you I can just as quick as I can.'

Reports reaching Irkens, though garbled and scarce, were in

sufficient volume to prime his instinct. Clearly the enemy was within minutes of securing the ridge on his left where the renewed bombardment had caused more damage than ever before in this battle. It was likely that Weber's Sixth Company was dissolving under fire, broken in spirit. Weber's last message had been filled with gloom. First reports told of fusiliers returning fire with their old asperity, but soon came news of men who fired once for effect and then raised their hands in surrender. Irkens shrugged. He would never know who had deserted even if their names were quoted. That was a fundamental difficulty with the supply of unknown replacements who flowed like water over falls, never to be registered, not to be conserved, and who were lost quickly to view.

The thunder of the ridge battle bubbled and swelled. Irkens's battle-tried senses traced its gradual shift deeper into his territory. It helped him make up his mind. Starved of information though he was, the moment for counter-attack had come. Wait too long and the enemy would be digging in and, in no time at all, too strong to be ejected. Moreover, with every minute that passed, the Fifth Company would be that much less likely to respond. An immediate counter-attack might even rescue significant numbers of front-line defenders who had resisted capture. Hold the line for a few hours longer and, who could tell, reinforcements might miraculously arrive. Still more miraculously, night might fall in time and with it permission could come to retire to a safer locality. It was, in any event, a fortuitous moment to act. Von Schilling reported that contact with two of the gun positions in rear had been re-established. A measure of artillery fire could be provided in support of the advancing Fifth Company and its single assault gun. Already the battalion's mortars were engaging some weird enemy tanks in the minefield. It was comforting to be hitting back again. Upon his order the guns opened against the ridge, ploughing positions which, a moment before, had been held by his own men (and which might still be inhabited by some of them). Thus German shell fire began to mingle with that of the Americans on the north side of the ridge while the British guns lengthened their range and searched southward into the German lines – raking the area where Fifth Company was beginning its advance to the counter-attack – turning both sides of the ridge into a cauldron.

Irkens emerged from the cellar and looked left for a sight of his battalion's saving throw. Frequently, as a junior officer, he had experienced what the leader of Fifth Company was now enduring – the anxiety of a young leutnant urging his men, cold with apprehension, into the artillery's wrack; casting them among an uplifted foe who was all the more formidable in the euphoria of success; trying, somehow, to raise their spirits from a trough to match and overcome an enemy already riding the crest of a wave. He recalled how often, as a company commander, he had doubted the wisdom of reflex counter-attacks – the ones which went in because the book demanded it even when the factors of terrain and numbers, both so dear to German tactical practice, were adverse. The fallacy of projecting an intact, reserve sub-unit into chaos when common sense suggested the desirability of preserving it for use on stronger ground at a more appropriate moment, was undeniable. As a platoon commander he had criticized company commanders for asking the impossible; as a company commander he had accused battalion commanders of slavish subservience to stereotyped regulations. Now, as a battalion commander, he reacted in precisely the same way as his predecessors and obeyed the deep-seated tactical doctrine of his army because he could envisage no other way of keeping the initiative or holding his battalion sector together. Instinctively he believed that to relinquish the offensive was tantamount to surrender.

21 The Grapple

When Oberfusilier Braun and Staedler saw Davis's platoon breasting the slope, they directed a well-controlled squirt of machine-gun fire in that direction and then plunged for cover, dragging the gun and its ammunition to an alternative location. These were the ingrained movements of professional soldiers culled from training and experience, theirs the burst which bisected Trefall and made the enemy advance waver. But when next Braun raised his head to continue the engagement it was to find danger already too close for comfort. Coming on remorselessly the enemy fired from the hip at thirty metres range. It was almost too late for him to stop them. Only his comrades to the flank could do that – as in the old days, some eighteen months ago, they would unswervingly have done. But dilution of the German infantry with too much foreign blood and lower-grade leaders had eroded their determination. To his left he saw a figure in field grey stand up, hands raised. Hope drained from his veins and guts. He, too, impulsively, climbed to the surface, lifted his hands, cried '*Kamerad, Kamerad*' and prayed for leniency. Nothing like this would he have contemplated happening on the Russian front. There you fought to the ultimate conclusion against opponents who behaved like animals. The British and Americans, he was led to believe, assimilated the civilization of Western culture such as his own and would be strict in recognizing the rules of war.

Parker gave a cry of exultation as the enemy surrendered and

shouted to his section, 'Come on ...' But Carver was quicker. These creatures he associated with Trefall's killers, who had slain without compunction when it was expedient and now, when all was lost, begged for mercy. With tempestuous hatred he swung the Bren from the hip and distributed a full magazine of twenty-eight rounds, mowing them down with a hot, venomous satisfaction. Eighteen hours ago he would not have done it. Now, in the charge to the hedge, over the still twitching bodies, it was Carver who took the lead and he who was first in the prone position behind his Bren, hunting for fresh targets beyond, among the copse. Contemptuously he ignored Parker's gasping remonstrance of disgust.

Parker, of course, judged standards of violence by the Queensberry Rules of fisticuffs; he was trained to recognize the moment at which punishment must stop. Yet this was not the occasion for complaint: there are no intervals between rounds in a grapple to the death. Carver was his most powerful agent of destruction, a good Bren gunner with his blood up just when the enemy might be expected to recoil upon them. Ever a realist, Parker gave Carver pride of place in the tight circle of defence it was his duty to form on their objective. There was a demand for urgency. The bark of grenades exploding to their right informed him that the platoon had yet to secure its objective. He had a momentary glimpse of Davis leaping down among some entrenchments. After that nothing was to be seen. The entire platoon seemed to vanish.

Garston's right-hand platoon, encroaching into the American sector, also recognized the attraction of relative safety which might, paradoxically, be found within the enemy lines. By means of their unnatural silence the enemy beckoned. Nevertheless, it could be an ambush, although instinct told them safety was assured. Thirty yards from the crest they yearningly reached for the objective – and at that moment the first American shells landed. To a man the platoon gasped as if the first spray from a cold shower of water had hit them. A momentary pause, almost a shudder, and then like swimmers thrown into a strong and icy current, they struck out boldly for the nearest dry land, racing (those who could) for shelter in the enemy trenches. What Callendar had applauded as an act of cool, calculated courage was, in reality, a reflex escape bid. Moreover, what appeared to the onlookers as total disaster was not entirely so. The first shells fell slightly to one side into soft ground which baffled their detonation, directing the bulk of splinters upwards instead of sideways. Before the next batch could arrive those men still on their feet – and only three had fallen – had covered the ground and were tumbling into the German trenches. Private John Paterson jumped feet first onto Fusilier Ulrich Doppler's head.

'*Kamerad,*' cried Ulrich, who had long ago lost interest in fighting.

'Blimey,' replied Paterson who was in no posture to use a rifle in the confines of the trench, and whose bayonet was still in its scabbard. But quickly taking charge, 'OK, Jerry, hand over your gun.'

Though Doppler spoke no English the order was plain enough. He pointed to the rifle standing in one corner of the pit, but before Paterson could seize it yet another body rolled in on top of them. Private Ernie Wright had been hit in the face by a splinter: blood flowed profusely from a long gash.

'Hold it, Ernie,' said Paterson, and fumbled in his trouser pocket for a field dressing. The German was quicker and already producing bandages and lint. Together, without speaking a word, they dressed the groaning man's wound, Paterson marvelling at the gentleness with which the German handled his enemy. When the job was done he looked straight at the German (the first he had ever met), reached into his battledress blouse and drew out a tin.

'You're a good bloke, Jerry,' he said. 'Have a fag.'

The same sort of anti-climax was enacted in the other German trenches. Eight leaderless men happily surrendered to British soldiers who were only in search of shelter. Thereafter the German Sixth Company, broken in front by the Americans and in centre by the British, could muster barely a few details in rear of the crest – details who knew nothing of what had happened at the front and who cared somewhat less. Leaders in distant places – the Simcoxes, Callendars and Irkenses of the hierarchy – could no longer influence the depths of the grapple nor alter its outcome.

Even commanders in intermediate proximity to the points of impact were slaves to circumstances. Garston, for example, closely though he and his headquarters moved with his company's leading platoons, was isolated by a dense confluence of drifting smoke and dust eddying among the thick green *bocage*. He fostered a reasoned hope that Davis's platoon was in possession of the left sector, but the fate of the right-hand platoon, swallowed by that pulverizing artillery delivery, remained inscrutable. Quite by chance he stumbled upon a section from the reserve platoon who had delicately held back from the advance and thus remained, fortuitously, uncommitted to the shambles. Incorporating them into his Company HQ along with the team of two who carried the radio for Thornton he headed up what could only be described as a corridor of unnatural calm – a passage which, by some freak, remained temporarily untouched by shellfire and which led to where Davis was trying to reorganize his platoon. In mutual astonishment they began to assemble – Davis exploring leftward to discover Parker and his section and bring them into the orbit of his defensive plan; Garston arriving and directing Davis to continue the advance into the copse no matter how unhealthy it might seem.

A flail tank had reached them and was tentatively firing high-explosive shells among the copse's undergrowth. Climbing upon its engine deck, Garston asked the commander to accompany them among the trees.

'No can do, sir,' was the uncompromising reply, with what Garston took to be an undertone of satisfaction. 'With this bloody boom we'll stick between trees even if we don't lose a track on stumps.'

It was on the tip of Garston's tongue, recognizing a rehearsed answer, to give a direct order, telling the wretched fellow to comply with a senior officer. But he checked the impulse and temporized.

'All right then. Stay here but put down a good dose of fire to the left and make bloody sure nothing interferes from that quarter while we go through this copse. Understood?'

'Yessir.' It was glib and they both knew it.

Thornton was waiting and so was Davis and his men. These he could trust.

'I'm in Strength Five contact with my chaps,' said the Gunner, 'and the whole regiment is now in support of you. But they say there's a bit of an ammo shortage so we may have to ration things. Sorry! Meantime they'll give three rounds per gun to the other side of the copse when you want it.'

'Thanks, Paul', said Garston with a broad smile. 'Better service than I got from that useless tank man over there. Never mind.' Then to Davis, 'Ready to go, Frank?'

'Ready, sir.'

'All right then! Paul! Your three rounds please and then let's go.'

Warily he led them deeper into the copse, endeavouring to make haste overcome caution in order to reach the other side before the expected enemy counter-stroke developed; grateful for the thunder of 25-pounder 'crumps' rending the far side; flinching as two random shells detonated high in the trees with a tearing air-burst; tense at the prospect of a sudden ambush. Close at heel walked Thornton, his whole attention directed to calculating the orders to give should trouble flare from one direction or another, planning, even, the instructions for playing the mightiest trump of all – the Uncle Target of the whole division's guns which, the CO had told him on the air, might be granted without demur. For the gunners had appreciated, with the infantry brigadier's concurrence, that this, perhaps, was the culminating stage of the battle.

Here and there the enemy declared himself - with snap shots from frightened marksmen and a lobbed stick-grenade or two - none to cause much harm but each a hindrance. Their opponents' habit of surrender became contagious, quite unchecked by Weber who had lost touch with his men in every sense. Weber himself was captured by Parker close to the crest line and escorted to Garston who placed him under guard in the German Company Commander's original command post. It was a symbol of mutual tactical agreement that each chose the same locality. Though radio contact had been lost with Simcox, Thornton managed to pass the extent of their success through Gunner radio channels so that, within a few minutes of its accomplishment, Simcox was aware that little more than a score of his men had reached the objective and had gained observation beyond. If it occurred to him that the despised radio was the channel for this vital news, he probably put it down to Gunner Black Magic and not the performance of men who were determined to make radio function.

Thornton crawled to where Parker, at a hedge junction, was disposing half a dozen men on the edge of the copse a few yards beyond the crest. Over-optimistically, the artillery officer hoped to find new horizons - an unscreened panorama with targets galore upon it. As usual the range of vision was restricted by the immense hedges to a hundred yards at most, and in places to half that distance. He thought he could see movement taking place through one thin patch, but could not be positive. Nevertheless, here he might fight the next battle and adapt his resources to make the best of things. Over the radio he began calling for shots ranged along the line of the farther hedge. There a defensive concentration of shellfire might be crucial in warding off a German counter-attack. Discounting Parker's little section and knowing how small was Garston's reserve, he felt convinced that guns alone would save the day - and trusted that, in this appallingly complex country, he had read the map correctly, judged the range well and thus called for an accurate shoot. The first ranging round, when it arrived, could confirm or deny his competence.

There was a disturbance to Garston's right – by Sergeant Pollack's platoon as it happened – heading in some trepidation, at Briggs's command, for the crest. Lacking fire support, except for what the remainder of Company 'B' could provide from a single 60mm mortar and small-arms fire, they, like Garston's men, enjoyed an easy passage, reaching the crest and beginning to dig in. Tersely, on the SCR 536 walkie-talkie radio, Pollack reported his arrival. With pleasure and relief he watched two Sherman tanks emerge from the orchard and waddle towards them. That they were British neither registered nor, if it had, would have worried him. Corporal Carter did not care either, for he was intent on seeking cover for his squad located to the platoon's left flank. One tank looked much the same as another to him. Private Novak, nursing his anglophobia, might have been unhappy but just then he, too, was engrossed in scooping a foxhole, somewhat astonished at finding himself alive and unharmed after two separate attacks in one day and rather delighted with his personal performance. For some reason he could not fathom he felt positive enthusiasm and pride in what he and the squad had achieved. It was an original and warming experience.

From behind the thin line of Anglo-American khaki at the crest reinforcements dribbled to their assistance. Snow, who had stationed himself at the mouth of the minefield gap, was urging on Robertson's 1 Troop, and calling forward the first of the Fireflies too, as buttresses for the anti-tank defence. To his right, without need of orders, Partridge's tanks detached themselves from the orchard and also made for the crest. That pleased Snow and prompted the decision to advance again himself, in order to impose his authority at the centre of his squadron's domain. Half-formed in his mind was a plan to turn left-handed in due course and eliminate, with point-blank shooting from the rear, that last remaining enemy resistance at Vertefeuille Farm. But at that moment there came an intensification of enemy artillery fire, pounding the crest line ahead. 'One thing at a time,' Snow silently chided himself, and aloud to his driver, 'Advance down the flail track and keep tight to where the others went.'

Paul Thornton was the first to catch a glimpse of the German infantry as they flitted past a gap in the distant hedge. Perhaps there was some sort of vehicle, too, but he could not be positive. In any case he was scanning hard for the fall of that first ranging round, the word 'Shot' having just come through his headphones to notify its dispatch. Everything happened at once. With a soul-rending moan mortar bombs clumped all around and about, a long raking burst of German machine-gun fire (no mistaking that searching rasp) sheared the foliage overhead, and his solitary ranging round detonated somewhat vaguely in the distance: he barely detected it as a faint haze funnelling skyward. Without waiting for interpretation Thornton appreciated that this was the beginning of the expected enemy counter-attack, and was shouting 'Uncle Target! Uncle Target!' into the microphone, calling for it on the same range and bearing as that taken by the single, ill-defined ranging shot. The outcome might well be imperfect but, allowing for the spread of every gun in the division, it should plaster the enemy in the desired manner.

Unfortunately it might also land among themselves.

With a flurry, orders poured through gunner command posts to 25-pounder troops and thence to the guns themselves where the swift routine of relay and counter-check was observed with precise efficiency by gun commanders whose only distraction was speed. Ammunition numbers, already sweated and fatigued from the morning's labours, were exhorted or bullied to fresh endeavours. But the supply of shell was limited because the lorries, making their way to the battery positions, had been delayed in the traffic-crowded roads. There was insufficient ammunition for a prolonged effort by the whole division, though the nearest trucks were close and under instructions to drive straight to the gun positions. Nevertheless the essential demands of an 'Uncle Target' had to be met, even at the expense of every shell in the pits. Inside three minutes word percolated back to Thornton.

'Ready,' announced Pratt, the Adjutant, with the arrogance he reserved for these occasions.

Well within bogey time, it had nevertheless seemed a long wait for Thornton, even though he had been busy warning Garston. And Garston, ignoring the enemy bombardment, had stood up, shouting instructions to those of his men within reach and earshot. Davis, too, took a risk and dodged amid the German shell bursts, telling his men to keep their heads up in observation. They paid for this. A flash from the gateway in the far corner of the field announced the intervention of an assault gun. The high-explosive round, bursting in the bank, killed a rifleman.

Garston saw it happen and warned his PIAT man to be ready to engage an enemy tank, well knowing, as he did so, that the target was beyond the range of an assured hit in a situation where, if the first shot missed, they were all doomed. In his imagination he visualized the enemy piling up on the other side of the field. From far to the right he heard a long burst from a tank machine-gun and guessed - correctly - that one of the Shermans had opened fire. But at what? Dearly would he have liked to speak with the tank commander and point him in the direction of that menacing enemy tank. But he did not know which tank it was and therefore he was ignorant of its radio call-sign. In any case his radio contact with the tank squadron was dead.

Of these things Sergeant Pollack saw nothing, though Corporal Carter, lying closer to the British and thus nearer the impending counter-attack than his platoon commander, was dimly aware of sinister shapes accumulating to the south. Above the engine tick-over of the Sherman tank nearby, he could hear another engine, of deeper note, revving and straining somewhere to the front. When the Sherman suddenly sent its long burst of machine-gun fire·skimming the hedge he tensed and shouted a warning.

'Watch out, that guy's seen something we ain't. Check your mags and weapons. Hey, Hoffman, get to the hedge intersection on the left. Something's coming that way.'

They cleared leaves away to form embrasures, dreading what might appear but irrevocably committed to the fight. Helplessly, Carter reasoned that, having come this far, there seemed no point in going back. The revival of faith acquired by Novak somehow absorbed them as a community. It had come to their knowledge that they were capable of taking on anybody – even those vaunted krauts. For the first time they actually spoiled for a fight before it began.

22 Counter-Attack

With well-rehearsed precision Company Five walked to its task, aided by a shaky optimism that their work would be easy; inspired by the truly stupendous volume of fire which had so recently fallen on the enemy who had occupied Sixth Company's territory. It was not for them to know that the main contribution had come from the Americans firing in error. Warily tense and yet uplifted by knowledge of an assumed superior prowess, their leading platoon closed on the hedge and saw the assault gun manoeuvre at the gate and open fire. The other two platoons, in lines by sections, breasted the bank, struggled through the hedgerow, picked up formation again and advanced in an orderly manner to the rescue of their comrades. Meanwhile, as of routine, the first platoon laid down small-arms fire to their flanks, augmenting the mortar and artillery fire which was already falling.

At once, from the shattered copse, came a smattering of bullets – perhaps from a tank, since the burst was long and frequently laced with tracer. According to drill they flung themselves down, were collected by shouts from their leaders and again rose, section by alternating section, to sprint ten yards and drop, once more, waiting for the others to take their chance. Here and there a man fell untidily, stayed still or writhed in agony. Mathematical probabilities indicated, however, that using these tactics they could reach their objective in sufficient strength to accomplish their mission – providing, that was, the hostile fire no more than doubled itself.

The single shell which ominously had fallen close to the leading platoon acted as warning, to the veterans, of what was to follow. Veer to right and left of its mark as they did it was too much to hope for total escape from bombardment. And that which fell exceeded anything they had experienced before. A downpour of metal and explosives smothered them with flying debris, a drum fire which reduced minds to incoherence as well as pulverizing bodies. From among the leading platoons, but a single section was separated from the beaten zone and then merely by a metre or so. For the remainder of the company, including those who had straggled to the hedge and the mortar men who had set up their tubes nearby, there was no escape. Caught in the open they were virtually obliterated by the Uncle Target. Those few who escaped unwounded were utterly spent – deafened by the blasting and mentally numbed. In less than a minute the assault gun received two hits besides a liberal spattering by splinters. The commander, in desperation, gave an order to reverse and turn round, but in so doing exposed the dim outline of the vehicle's hull to a British tank he had not observed. A single shot penetrated the assault gun's hull and at once she was burning. Nobody got out.

For five minutes it rained shells. After it was over the survivors could hardly hear let alone muster the wit to take sensible evasive action. The lightly wounded began to stagger away and were overtaken by the unscathed minority who fled in a blind panic. Only a few samaritans turned to succour the wounded. Bullets flew thick and fast among the Germans, fired by the enemy who lined the copse they had, just a few minutes ago, so confidently set out to secure. The notion of surrender simply did not occur to the survivors' confused minds. Those who were not killed or wounded feigned death: a field once alive with moving figures became a cratered carpet dotted with grey bundles which lay still, writhed, moaned or screamed.

Irkens had seen them go, had read the ominous noises of battle and at once realized the outcome. When the enemy gunfire ceased he re-entered the cellar to find Barentz with his face set and pale. He understood. The Sixth Company no longer existed. Therefore, to all intents and purposes, the battalion was finished.

Its remaining strength was founded only upon a few scattered details of the Fourth Company on the right (at that very moment fully engaged on all sides) and his own headquarters, supported by a thin artillery contribution. Of armoured vehicles none were left, of anti-tank guns perhaps one - nobody knew. They were in pawn to the enemy, and out of all contact with higher headquarters. Irkens assumed, therefore, that Regimental, and probably Divisional, HQ were also shattered.

A good CO is selected for duty, not heroics. Heavily Irkens gave instructions to Barentz, loudly enough for all in the cellar to hear.

'We will defend this locality until nightfall and then, with Company Four, retire. Leutnant Barentz, you will organize a perimeter guarding this farm, using every available man. I will try to reach Company Four and bring them back. If I do not return you have my permission to break out southward at nightfall.'

There was no discussion. The gravity of the situation was obvious to them all and this plan offered a measure of hope. Barentz called for Hauptfeldwebel Loring, the senior man present, and began detailing tasks as Irkens set forth on his mission.

The loom of the crest line threatened Irkens. Only the partly sunken lane, whose course he had followed that morning (was it so short a time ago?) seemed safe, and so this was the path he took in the general direction of Vertefeuille Farm. Here and there he met stragglers whom he directed to the rear. From Pankewitz and his crew he heard of the destruction of the Jagdpanther. Politely he thanked them for their efforts and also directed them back. As he came in sight of the forward slope and the ruined farm beyond, he recognized the hopelessness of the situation. Khaki figures flitted stealthily through the trees, to the right, the front and, no doubt, behind him. From within the farm came the sound of brisk, short-range combat. He turned aside and found himself confronted by a short man in khaki pointing a small sub-machine gun in his direction.

Neither spoke. The gun was level but silent. He raised his hands and stood still. Another man appeared and took his pistol.

For him the war was over, and in that moment of release from responsibility it suddenly occurred to him that he was flatly devoid of emotion, though trembling.

23 The Duel

The arrival of a friendly tank among the outer ruins of Vertefeuille Farm counteracted Harry Spriggs's worst fears. Moreover he had judged correctly that, since the attack on his part of the front had stalled, it was more than likely to be renewed elsewhere. In this division the reinforcement of failure was frowned upon - or so he was led to believe. Naturally ninety-nine per cent of his attention was focused upon the narrow boundaries defined by the farm's broken masonry, uprooted trees and torn shrubbery, and within those confines he had come to identify an opponent with style. The exchanges of the past hour or more had revealed a pattern of sporadic, though precisely co-ordinated, enemy resistance. Nearly every enemy shot had been timed for critical occasions and seemed to be aimed with clear purpose, as though directed by a single brain, if not from the same person. The effect upon his platoon had been unnerving. It was sapping their resistance. His losses were mounting. Thus he came to link the enemy's determined performance with one fleeting figure he had occasionally glimpsed. Near where the bazooka had fired he had seen him; close from where an accurate burst of machine-gun fire had come he had observed him again - and also during a sharp exchange of grenades which had wounded one of his men. Spriggs felt challenged to a duel with this man and, for want of a satisfactory alternative, took it up. Methodically he disposed his men for limited tasks, posting them like guns at a grouse shoot, each to his own butt. From the tank commander he requested overhead machine-gun cover for himself in his self-appointed roles of stalker and beater. This took a long time to arrange for the threat from this killer in his midst redoubled caution and slowed down the passing of orders.

Kramer had not the slightest realization that such close attention was being paid to him. With blinkered determination he struggled to fulfil his instructions - to goad, persuade and compel a scattered handful of frightened German fusiliers to bend to his will. Bitterly he harangued them in his efforts to make them overcome fear and compel them to fight: angrily he cursed them when they failed. By repeated changes of location he accomplished a double purpose - distracting the enemy as well as imposing discipline upon his company by supervision. With close attention to essentials he took the lion's share of work and, incidentally, subjugated his own fears.

The arrival of the tank had rather shaken his confidence and his hopes of killing it had been undermined because Hengst and his panzerfaust were no longer to be found. Ducking among rubble and following covered ways, shaped haphazardly by the bombardment, he found, instead, two cowering riflemen. These he appointed as a personal escort, telling them to keep him in sight and to fire to their front in an attempt to frighten the enemy. Yet, as he set out again, a shot whacked close above his head and a stream of bullets rapped a wall, generating a shower of brick dust. Spriggs had opened his account in their duel and the tank had joined in.

Spriggs had at last obtained a proper look at the German leader and recognized him as such since he seemed to be giving orders. He fired a fraction of a second after Kramer moved, however, and missed. Obviously the tank had done no better, for its machine-gun fire had traversed in the opposite direction to the German's escape. But now, at last, he had a rough idea of his quarry's location, and could plan a systematic search. He was again under fire himself from single shots to the front - unaimed, it seemed, but discouraging. Sliding through rubble on his belly, he took cover behind a short wall and then ran its length, seeking a safer position of observation.

Just in time he saw a man, perhaps the one he hunted, slinking round the next corner near the farm's midden, trailing what looked like a drainpipe. He doubled through the wrecked outhouses that ran parallel with the midden, making for the next open space, where he hoped to have clear shot. It was empty. Behind and to his left he heard a renewed fusilade of shots and a cry of pain. That, he thought, could hardly be from the man he sought. It must have been an engagement involving his 'grouse party' and yet another of the enemy. He waited on one knee at a corner, rifle at the ready, panting a little. Perhaps the enemy would come to him.

Hengst had been found by Kramer skulking in a pig-stye and was bullied outside. Near the midden they climbed a pile of masonry, making for an upper pinnacle, to obtain a view of the tank. They were not disappointed. Its turret, traversing slowly, left to right, was a bare thirty yards off, its gun side on. This was his chance, when the crew was looking elsewhere. Hengst raised the clumsy weapon but at that very moment he saw the turret suddenly traverse fast in his direction. Scarcely taking aim he presssed the trigger and ducked, the hasty action sending the missile flying above the turret to explode harmlessly out of sight.

'Idiot,' stormed Kramer. They jumped down as a shell from the tank slammed among the rubble, covering them with dirt and opening a gash in Hengst's head. Kramer cursed again. He should have done the job himself.

Spriggs swore too. He had distinctly told that tank commander to lay off high explosive among the farm buildings. Fragments had spattered around him and the explosion, though deflected by brickwork, had made his ears ring, partially deafening him. The corner of the short wall offered a view of the midden, and he made for this. In so doing he brought himself into full view of Kramer, who had abandoned Hengst and the now useless panzerfaust, and was rooting like a pig for grenades where some had been dumped the day before.

Kramer fired from the hip, the sub-machine gun raising dust near the heels of the running Spriggs. It cost half a valuable magazine for no clear result. Moreover, for the first time, the sensation of being hunted intruded upon Kramer. He looked left and right for room for manoeuvre, searching, too, for a hiding place from which to catch his opponent at a disadvantage. Moving stealthily he rounded another corner.

With his heart pounding and his knees weak Spriggs leant against a wall and took a breather. The heel of his boot felt loose and, upon examination, he found it hanging off having being struck by a bullet. That bloody Hun was good but, thank God, not such a hot shot. He must shift again and this time finish the job. Above was a window, probably the last at upper level to survive the bombardment. Providing no German was already in that room it offered a superb, commanding position. It would be risky entering such an obvious vantage point but it seemed a risk worth taking since the Hun he sought could not yet be there. Nobody else seemed to matter at that moment. Gingerly he mounted a rotten, torn stairway. The door was off its hinges. He took a deep breath, darted through and backed against the opposite wall, his rifle at the ready, but silent. It was important not to draw attention to his arrival. But it had been dangerous. In the drill manner he should first have tossed in a grenade and opened fire as he entered. Nevertheless the room was empty. Spriggs crawled to the window and cautiously raised his head above the sill. The ruins lay below him and beyond them the British lines. From there he saw groups of men approaching and a tank bustling among them. Then the German appeared, creeping into sight round the nearest corner.

Spriggs had killed and was accustomed to ordering men to kill. Never had he done so dispassionately, no matter how far distant and indistinct the victim. On the first occasion, after giving a routine fire order, which virtually amounted to sentence of death upon three Germans near Hill 112, he had actually jerked out an involuntary withdrawal of the command. It had been too late. He had despised himself both for exhibiting a chicken heart and at the same time for taking life. The act had got easier with practice though never yet had he killed dispassionately. Now it seemed he must, for the German was apparently quite unaware of his peril. Spriggs raised the rifle and took careful aim. Simultaneously he experienced an extraordinary mixture of disgust and weariness at the whole business of war and the waste of slaughtering a man

whose prowess he had come to respect. He contemplated taking
yet another risk. The decision was made. His finger tightened
with its first pull on the trigger. Then he shouted some of the
only German words he knew.

'*Hand hoch.*'

Perhaps, felt Kramer, much later on reflection, he should have
persevered to the end and disobeyed that command. But he, too,
was tired, and knew in that instant that nothing more could be
achieved. Maybe he had known it all along. And anyway, at that
moment life seemed rather precious. He froze, dropped his gun
and raised his hands.

To Codrington, arriving to take personal command, the sight
of Spriggs idly escorting a single prisoner was most irritating. In
a state of tension induced by the fate of his company, and
imbued with the single-minded aim of restoring its fortunes, his
temper boiled over.

'For God's sake, Harry,' he cried. 'Don't bother about prisoners. Mop up the rest of the farm. I've got more chaps coming on to help. Now's the time to get at 'em. Leave that bastard to private soldiers.'

Spriggs recoiled. 'Look,' he shouted, 'I'm the one who's run this show so far and I'm the one who'll finish it. This bastard,' pointing to Kramer, 'was king-pin here, or I'm a Dutchman. With him out of the way the rest may pack it in any moment. For Christ's sake, Major, lay off and let me do things my way. Here, you look after him.'

Codrington regarded his subordinate with blank astonishment and in mutual anger. A hot retort came to his lips but would have been wasted, for Spriggs had already turned away and was shouting to a Bren gunner. 'You, sonny, come with me. The rest of you give fire on the buildings to the right – five rounds each.' With an effort they complied, shaking off exhaustion, moving once more with rhythm and an athletic spring.

Codrington fell silent and retired in the direction of the tank, taking Kramer with him at pistol point, and watched the ex-sergeant-major organizing a copybook house-clearing operation. Fire support from one group helped another to reach its assault position adjacent to some door, window or bunker. Then a grenade would be tossed into the room followed, after its explosion, by a machine-gunner who dashed in, backed against a wall and sprayed everything in sight. Twice the process was used but before the third attempt a dishevelled and wild-eyed German appeared with his hands raised high. Immediately they heard repeated calls of *'Kamerad'* and more Germans emerged from obscure hiding places. Codrington grinned with delight. 'C' Company had taken at least part of its first objective. He heard voices behind him. The rest of the company were arriving at the trot, led by the sergeant-major. He felt vindicated.

24   Withdrawal

At headquarters of II/431st Infantry Battalion there were soldiers suffering from shock: the brain of the battalion suddenly
found itself severed from the body as the stream of messages,
which had been passing to its extremities, ceased. All at once the
headquarters staff were brought face to face with the practical
certainty of close, physical combat. No longer were they
segregated from the brutalities of the front line. To Barentz and
Hauptfeldwebel Loring, who had both graduated to the highest
echelon of a battle unit by virtue of character and ability and had
survived because of generous slices of luck, the situation was
familiar, of course. Nor was it a totally fresh experience for
Hauser, although in the past he had usually avoided close
involvement. As a signaller, selected by virtue of a higher in-
tellect than that of the common fusilier, he had managed to
achieve a sort of remoteness from brawling. To the cooks and
clerks, however, most of whom were barely recruits, exposure to
direct enemy fire was abrupt and unnerving in its unexpected-
ness.

On occasions such as these Loring was at his best, posting the
men to their trenches with a mellow mixture of brusqueness and
understanding that had matured in ten years' infantry service.
Barentz left him to it and deliberated the next move. Though
Irkens had left scarcely any latitude outside his demand that they
stand and fight, there must surely come a moment for change,
particularly if the conditions worsened and Irkens did not return.

For in his heart Barentz was convinced that his commander had gone for ever. He had seen tears in Baumler's eyes when Irkens had departed to rescue the rest of the battalion. Barentz had heard the man say, 'We'll not see him again. There goes the best master we'll ever have.' He had rounded on Baumler and cursed him for a defeatist. Privately, however, he respected the older man's insight.

Men in grey were running towards them – some the drift-wood of panic, others those whom Irkens had met and directed to safety. Pankewitz and his crew were there, answering Barentz's questions about what they had seen, and then coming under the command of Loring who fitted them into the defence. Last to arrive was von Schilling accompanied by his signallers, carrying between them the radio set that still maintained contact with the gun batteries. At once it became possible to maintain a semblance of local artillery protection. Von Schilling began chanting orders and co-ordinates to the gun positions. That was reassuring. Barentz would have been happier still if Dettinger, the mortar's forward observer, had escaped but there was no news of him so they laid a new telephone cable direct to Thoma's mortars and assumed direct control themselves.

Shells began to land nearby, bullets whistled overhead, tank tracks' rattle and engine mutter got louder in the *bocage* to their front. The men gripped their weapons. Loring went the rounds, uttering fresh exhortation. Baumler crouched close by Hauser, suspiciously studying a companion who muttered to himself in anguish.

'Shut up,' he demanded 'You have not seen nothing yet. Don't you remember the Russians? They were worse than these English. We stopped them.'

Hauser ignored it. His mind was a whirl of conflicting loyalties and emotions. Four shells landed in quick succession nearby, showering them with debris. There was a wail of agony from the opposite end of the farm where a man had been hit. Loring strode in that direction, to assess the damage. By the sound of it, he thought, the injured man could not be badly hurt – the noisy ones rarely were. As he disappeared from view Hauser moved to follow.

'Stay where you are,' shouted Baumler.

'Stay if you like,' came the reply. 'Not me! We'll be here for good if we don't watch out.' Hauser had taken a final decision upon impulse. He must escape. He climbed out of the trench and ran.

Baumler had long ago lost scruples. Years of Army discipline had hardened his dim imagination and implanted a strict sense of duty and behaviour. Without the slightest hesitation or remorse he took aim at Hauser's back and shot the man down. He would have been more disturbed had it been a sick animal in need of destruction.

The shot attracted Barentz. 'What did you see?' he asked Baumler, supposing that the enemy were in sight.

Baumler pointed to Hauser's corpse. 'He bolted. I warned the Major. He said he would watch.' Then with simple reproach, 'It would not have happened if the Major had been here.'

There was nothing Barentz could say. He touched the man on the arm and returned to von Schilling.

The artillery officer had news and with it a question for Barentz. 'I have it from the batteries,' he announced, 'only five rounds per gun remain, and there is no hope of replenishment. Therefore we cannot shoot much longer. In any case the enemy have advanced so far on the right that the guns must soon retire or be overrun. I am to say that they can stay not much more than thirty minutes. Is there anything I can do in that time? Are there any special targets you wish me to engage? Perhaps, in the circumstances, you are thinking of withdrawing yourself?'

That final question was crucial to Barentz. Despite their perilous state, their lack of orders or information from Regimental HQ, their shortage of heavy weapon support, and their deficiency of reliable men, there was Irkens's last order to remember - and Irkens might return. Yet what was the point of defending ground which was already dominated and outflanked by the enemy? Irkens had commanded Barentz to hold until nightfall and Irkens must be obeyed - whether he returned or not. But by then it might be too late, they might be surrounded and captured. Irkens was not the sort to make a useless sacrifice. As sole surviving officer - assuming Irkens was lost - Barentz had now to make a new decision and bear in mind, too, the implied reproach from Baumler directed at anybody who deserted Irkens. Barentz had also respected Irkens as a fine example of the best professional officers produced by the old army. Von Schilling was observing him closely and impatiently waiting. More enemy shells were falling. Vehicle noises grew louder near the crest. At one moment he thought he heard English voices. Calmly Barentz resolved the dilemma. Irkens was lost. If he were among them he would not condone the deliberate sacrifice of a cadre for a new battalion. Upon what remained at Battalion HQ something useful might be grafted in the future.

He called for Loring and jointly addressed the Hauptfeldwebel and von Schilling. 'We cannot stay here if the guns are leaving. We will withdraw to where the guns are now. The manoeuvre is to start in twenty minutes and follow the sunken lane we always use. We must keep the enemy quiet while we go. The mortars will begin an intensive bombardment of the entire crest line fifteen minutes before we leave until either all their bombs are gone or to within three minutes of departure. Then they will pack up and follow. The artillery will please bombard targets of opportunity which may appear in the meantime. Then, if possible, cover our retreat. Hauptfeldwebel, you will guide the men and ensure nothing is left to the enemy. What cannot be carried will be destroyed.'

He paused, examined their expressions closely, but found no clue to their feelings. Of whether they approved or disapproved, they gave no sign.

'Any questions?'

They stood silent. They were glad to go.

'Then I wish you good fortune. I will stay with von Schilling who, no doubt, will be the last to depart with myself.'

The two officers smiled at each other. It was ironic to find a Prussian and a Bavarian in close accord. How odd, thought von Schilling, that war and a common military code could close the rifts of history. He began speaking over the radio to the guns, at the same time keeping watch for enemy movement. Barentz was talking by telephone to mortar Obergefreiter Thoma, defining his tasks. Outwardly casual, Loring strolled among the men, briefing them for the withdrawal and dividing them into small parties, each under an NCO or senior soldier who had instructions to move in a prescribed order of march. The clerks were burning documents as fast as possible. Radio operators were preparing their sets for portage, smashing the pieces which could not be removed.

In the mortar pits Thoma had carried out a rough calculation of rates of fire in relation to the ammunition available. Every bomb - not very many, as he was quick to tell Barentz - was brought close to the weapons. The hazard of enemy bombardment, finding and hitting the sensitive bombs unprotected by blast walls, had to be accepted. In any case, the time to open fire was close. Each of the five tubes was aligned to its task. Thoma raised his hand and dropped it, calling, 'Fire'. This was their last effort. Ammunition numbers slaved at their work, handling bombs to the mortar's mouth, releasing them and ducking aside from the blast. Number 1s checked and rechecked their bubbles for accuracy as the battery churned out its load. In the distance they could hear the crumps on impact.

Five minutes before the first men were scheduled to depart, Loring reported everything in readiness to Barentz who, in the meantime, had checked that nothing of operational importance, such as secret documents, remained for the enemy. Satisfied that all was in readiness, he gave Loring permission to begin the retirement - a little prematurely perhaps. It might leave the mortars temporarily unguarded. Nevertheless it seemed unwise to tarry, especially since the enemy appeared quite oblivious to their presence or intentions. In any case, the mortars had ceased fire and he guessed they would be disassembling their pieces prior to moving off. Loring saluted and returned to lead the first party, calling upon the others to follow in turn. Picking up the theme, von Schilling gave orders for the firing of three rounds per gun beyond the crest line, hoping to catch enemy infantry in the open if they were forming up for a renewed advance.

Without regret they vacated the farm. When, at one frightening moment, a group of shells landed slightly to one side of the lane, they wondered if they had been spotted, but the *bocage* swallowed them like ghosts. Barentz, the last to depart, was relieved to see the mortar platoon, bent low under their loads, labouring through the lane ahead of him. Those valuable weapons at least would be denied to the enemy.

'Congratulations,' said von Schilling. 'I never thought we'd escape as cleanly as that.'

'Thank the *bocage*,' replied Barentz. 'It's as good as a Russian forest.'

'And thank the English too,' said von Schilling. 'We were lucky they did not get on to those mortars of yours.'

They turned the bend in the lane and saw the remnants of the battalion straggling to safety. How few they were – less than fifty strong perhaps. And how little they appeared to have achieved. Not a prisoner to show and not an acre of ground denied to the enemy. Their commander was lost with most of the men and all their assault guns and anti-tank artillery. For once in his life Barentz knew abject despondency. How much longer could this sort of thing go on?

25 March Past

When the guns came to the end of Thornton's crushing 'Uncle Target', and the smoke and dust had drifted away, it dawned upon those in local command of the Allied side that a crisis had been reached and passed, that the German defence was broken. It was not Thornton's reports, with their emphasis upon the decimation of the enemy counter-attack force, which persuaded them, but rather the abatement of stormy resistance signalized by a momentary, deathly stillness. Already on the left flank, where neighbouring units had advanced most deeply of all, German resistance was negligible. On the extreme right, too, among the 301st, there was such an apparent weakening that patrols were able to exploit almost unmolested. Joined with dying shots which reverberated through the ruins of Vertefeuille Farm, a sensation of relief, allied to German atrophy, crept across the frontage of the 1st East Hampshires. No longer did hostile mortars pummel the minefield. Already it was possible to move with safety in orchards and fields where, a few hours before, it would have been suicidal.

Along with discarded weapons, human debris was also being collected. The dead would be buried later, but now a search for the wounded was being made in long grass, aided by German prisoners and a few grim-faced Scots from the platoon of Gleneagles Highlanders, all of whom acted as stretcher bearers. The Scots had suffered badly, caught by cross-fire. The experience had struck deeper than if they had been working among their own nationality instead of with another tribe – the East Hampshires. As one of them put it to Codrington, 'We've nae wish to do it agin. We like best to fight with our ain.' It was one to add to a number of surprises experienced by Codrington that day.

The East Hampshire's Intelligence Officer, Buttonshaw, was questioning prisoners, looking for only one item of immediate information – the identity of the unit they had been fighting. His was a simple technique: pick the man who looked most amenable. In five minutes the information had been extracted from Ulrich Doppler and was on its way to Brigade HQ. Now it was confirmed that 326th Division still held the line. That item, added to the flow of confirmatory information pouring in across the breadth of the VIII Corps front, enabled senior intelligence officers to read the state of the enemy defences and draw the conclusion that an unreinforced opponent was on the verge of collapse. The most senior commanders at once felt justified in demanding additional efforts from the fighting soldiers, even those who had just been heavily engaged. From corps to division and from there to brigades and units ripples of accentuated encouragement spread out.

Krantsky answered the telephone, made notes and at once interrupted Simcox who was talking to Tranter.

'Colonel Simcox. My Colonel has fresh orders and would like to co-ordinate them with you. He thinks it might be easier to meet. What'll I say?'

'Let me speak to him,' said Simcox.

'Sorry, sir, that's impossible. He's up at the front and only in radio touch with the CP.'

'Right. Well, say I've fresh instructions, too; that I've got to open up wider gaps in the minefield for the use of follow-up troops and that I'm going now to the flail gap. Ask if he can meet me there in about quarter of an hour?'

Hurriedly Simcox's group loaded into jeeps and scout cars and drove for the rendezvous. Already there was the beginning of a traffic jam and soon it would be worse since another combat group, preponderant in tanks, was already on its way. Simcox had been told that a troop of Royal Engineers was arriving to extend the minefield clearance and marking, but he also ordered Keith Duncan to be ready to flail an additional lane just to be sure. His Regimental Police were already acting as traffic controllers though a detachment of Military Police from division should soon take over. From past experience Simcox could visualize the sort of jostling that would take place. The Military Police were better trained for handling that sort of situation. Even impatient senior officers thought twice before challenging the authority of an MP.

Simcox found Duncan and his flail standing in readiness at the minefield edge. 'This is work for the Sappers, you know, sir,' complained Duncan. 'My CO is keen that we should reserve ourselves for operational tasks.' Simcox was a little weary of obstructive tankmen and was curt, passing on an order which he claimed came from division. He also met Clive Foxton, 'A' Company's commander, and heard his excuses. With him Simcox was even more abrupt.

'Clive,' he said. 'I want your company on the other side of that minefield, deployed to the left of "B" Company on the crest in thirty minutes sharp.'

'But, Colonel, I don't know where half of them are in this *bocage* and. . .'

Simcox cut him short. 'Then bloody well find them and get cracking. In twenty minutes or less there's a regiment of tanks coming through this gap and you're to be out of the way. Moreover we are responsible for securing a start line for them on the crest and David Garston and his boys are in no state to do it on their own. Now stop arguing and do as I say.'

This, to Foxton, was a new Simcox. He saluted and was gone.

Sappers, swinging their mine-detectors, picket posts and tape, were being shown by Tranter where to start work. The Second-in-Command of Pentland Yeomanry drew up in his scout car. 'I've come to assess the state of the gap and liaise,' he told Simcox. 'There are a couple of our squadrons a field away.' Tranter introduced himself and they moved aside to confer. Krantsky was talking by radio to Callendar, sending directions on how to avoid the mines. In the minefield itself the East Hampshire's pioneers were clearing a path to Cain, as two

stretcher bearers stood by to remove the man who moaned and shook with uncontrollable fear.

From the crest line the noise of battle re-intruded as Barentz laid down his departing barrage. It in no way threatened those at the minefield, but it made them pause and glance hesitantly in the enemy direction, temporarily slowing them down by making them nervous. Officers looked questioningly towards Simcox and took comfort at his outward calm and plain determination. They turned to reassure their men, little knowing that, in fact, Simcox had scarcely heard the bombardment so highly concentrated was his mind on the task.

With a roar of exhaust, and a cloud of dust which Simcox deprecated, Callendar arrived, springing from his seat and walking briskly to Simcox whom he saluted with a broad grin.

'Sorry to be late,' he said, 'but there's been problems, big problems with the management.'

They shook hands.

'Well, we've had some of those ourselves, too,' said Simcox. 'I'm bound to say it came as something of a surprise when you unloaded that stonk on the crest line. Quite took the wind from our sails. But it did the trick. We made it.'

'Sorry about that,' said Callendar ruefully. 'I sure thought you realized that's what I had in mind. Just goes to show how little we know of each other. But as you say - we made it. I hope things aren't too bad for you?'

'Could be worse, though bad enough. "C" Company on the left took a beating. "B", the ones next to you, got away with it though, and remarkably lightly - thanks in no small measure to what your boys did. I'm grateful. And yours?'

Callendar quickly recapitulated his battalion's experience - which brought him to the point. 'My orders are to stand fast while our third battalion goes through on the right. The krauts are giving way, too, on that flank, but not as fast as on yours to the east. I guess the Air Corps did a good job there.'

'Sorry you'll not be coming with us, then,' said Simcox. 'I, too, have been told to consolidate here but I've got a warning order to be at one hour's notice after a tank regiment's gone through.' He pointed over his shoulder. 'That's them now.' A throb of engines and squeak of tracks was getting close.

'In that case it's likely we'll go on together,' said Callendar. 'We won't stay here long either. I pointed out to my Regimental Commander that it would be a shame to waste a good part-nership like ours.'

It was Simcox's turn to be pleased.

'Well, the drinks are on me this time,' he said. 'And I'd like to add how much help Bob Krantsky's been.' He reached into his jeep, drew out a haversack and extracted a bottle.

They stood to one side, clear of dust as the leading tanks of 'B' Squadron Pentland Yeomanry rolled into sight, lurching across the lane and entering the minefree passage that was, already, marked by white tape. Simcox and Callendar watched them with a sense of proprietorial pride in the joint achievements of their respective commands. They saw tanks, followed by infantry of the 5th Royal Dorsets, wending their way towards the crest, fanning out to exploit what the East Hampshires and 301st had made possible. To a flank they saw the flails beating a new path to expand the traffic flow. Culpepper joined them and was introduced to Callendar.

'I've orders to stay with you, Colonel,' he said, 'though my regiment now reverts to support of the Royal Dorsets. Paul Thornton will keep a fatherly eye on things until we're out of sight. Then he, too, is due for a rest. He did a good job today.'

'Thanks for reminding me, Brian,' said Simcox. 'We infantry rather take you gunners for granted and think we'd manage all right on our own. I've seen again today just how puny we are when it comes to the crunch.'

Callendar nodded. 'Sure. I've even got to admit that the tanks have their uses. Fact is, we'd still be stuck at this lane if the tankers hadn't been there.'

'But,' interposed Simcox, somewhat shocked by this betrayal of infantry's cause, 'you'll always need the man on his feet in the last analysis.'

A tank detached itself from the column and Douglas Ferriers jumped down from the turret.

'Glad to see you, Edward,' he greeted Simcox, and he too was introduced to Callendar. 'I'll be taking Philip Snow and his squadron back under command right away,' he went on. 'He seems not to have taken too bad a knock and I'll need him in reserve if we break loose. I gather he did a good job and I was pleased to listen to his style of handling things on the radio. Always did have promise, that young man.'

'Might make a good infantryman one day,' commented Simcox. 'No, indeed, he did a good job and I'm grateful. Doesn't give me much rope, tho',' he added.

Ferriers laughed and remounted, ordered his driver to advance, threading his way into the moving column that wended its way up the flail path. He gave a hard look at the burning flail and Grant's tank still heavily smoking. As he motored towards the crest, keenly scrutinizing his leading squadron as it deployed into battle formation, the infantry merging with *bocage* on either side, he could not help reflecting that, though the landscape was heavily pock-marked by shellfire, that was all. Here and there lay a body; in a hedge, to the left, stood what looked like a wrecked German anti-tank gun; a forlorn handful of prisoners was drifting back under escort, a group of stretcher bearers carrying their cargo to the rear – nothing so terrible, however, as reports on the air seemed to suggest might be the case. But his view, circumscribed by *bocage,* collected only small evidence of what had gone before – as Snow might have told him.

An infantry major he faintly recognized, through a coating of grime and sweat, was standing just short of the copse, speaking to his company sergeant-major. It was Garston – a thoroughly satisfied company commander. His company alone in the battalion had taken all their objectives, and done it by teamwork. True there had been failures. 'Now,' Garston thought, 'the tanks can take over where we leave off.'

Searching for easy access to the terrain into which his regiment was now penetrating, Ferriers moved right and halted on the boundary with the American sector. Already his leading tanks had breached the crest-line hedge and, with infantry escorts, were probing deeper into the *bocage*. Bursts of machine-gun fire notified their progress in harmony with radio talk which told of a tightly controlled, field by field, advance. To the right he saw American infantry emerging from cover, sidling up to one of Snow's tanks to engage in conversation with the crew who had dismounted to brew tea. A brisk trade was in progress. Private Novak, setting aside his prejudices, was bartering coffee for tea and spam for corned beef.

Another tank approached and Snow left its turret to cross and speak with Ferriers. Ferriers looked closely at his newest squadron commander, summing up his state of composure.

'Well done, Philip,' he said. 'Edward Simcox was pleased in his funny old way. Says you'll make a good infantryman yet!' They laughed. 'Sorry to hear about Sergeant Grant and his crew. Some of Simcox's chaps did a good job pulling them out of that minefield, by the way. Our doc has them in hand, you'll be glad to hear, but he doesn't give much hope for one of Grant's legs.'

Philip frowned. Grant had been a mainstay in the squadron, the type of younger NCO who got on well with the old hands and set a keen example to the youngsters.

'We'll miss him,' he said. 'I'm never sure how well we can replace men like him.'

'Oh come, Philip!' expostulated Ferriers. 'There'll always be more Grants, just as Ferriers have one day to be replaced by Snows and Snows by McBains. That's how the system works. Snap out of it. Don't let a few casualties depress you, especially ours. Look at the East Hampshires, now. Their Colonel's got to repair almost a complete company and, between you and me, has a problem with a company commander. We've nothing so awkward as that. Enough of that,' he went on. 'Now, this is how I see things working out for the next hour or so. There's about four hours' daylight remaining, and at this rate we'll be lucky to get anywhere near our objective by nightfall. You're in reserve from now and may not be needed again today. Stay at about thirty minutes' notice to move. Replenish by troops. I've seen to it that a couple of "A" Echelon trucks will be allowed through the minefield to reach you. They're coming up with the support company of the East Hampshires who've got to establish some sort of firm base in this locality. Fit your chaps into their scheme of defence. Now this is how I see the battle developing. . .' and he began to sketch a new course of events.

'One last thing,' he said, almost as an afterthought. 'I thought you handled your squadron well in the circumstances, but you took something of a chance sending those tanks unsupported up the right flank. Might have been OK if you'd been tied into a well-known infantry battalion - but you weren't.' Snow acknowledged the reproof without resentment, understanding that it was his Colonel's way of teaching. He recalled the catch phrase of so many exercise de-briefings, 'You never know it all'.

Overhead the skies had emptied of cloud and now he had the opportunity to watch the air forces at work, to see British Typhoon fighter-bombers arriving in flights of four, orbiting while a target was described to them by an air-force officer who spoke by radio from a tank that stood adjacent to Ferriers. One by one they peeled off to streak earthward, trailing smoke as their rockets discharged, the missiles flying ahead before each aeroplane turned away and raced for safety; the combined shriek and roar, interlaced with cannon fire, reverberated with the bang of rockets on impact. Puffs of smoke dotted the sky in their flight path when German light anti-aircraft guns haltingly shot back. But the effect was minimal, hits unrecorded.

The 25-pounders were advancing too, 'P' Battery's guns lumbering along the rutted minefield gap. Methodically they fanned out in the field and prepared to open fire, thus extending the range at which support could be given to the slowly advancing infantry and tanks; getting comfortably settled in daylight prior to the night-fighting that might come; accumulating ammunition for a prolonged engagement. First gun through the gap and first to unlimber from its tractor was Bastick's, the indefatigable sergeant chasing a tired crew into readiness for action well ahead of the others. No protective gun pits for them now. Open warfare had recommenced. Even the troop command post stood exposed to danger in the open, though its more cautious and less involved members were busy excavating trenches while signallers paid out cable to the guns and ammunition trucks delivered their loads. In due course the entire regiment would occupy this site.

As the afternoon wore on and fears of enemy repercussions dwindled, the crowd thickened. Carriers bearing insulated boxes containing a hot meal went forward to the East Hampshires. There was plenty to spare in 'C' Company at Vertefeuille Farm and not only because their numbers were sadly depleted. Several of the men suffered from mild shock and were repelled by food. Sleep claimed the majority, however, sleep or talk among those for whom psychological relief was best obtained by relating the events of the morning and by letting off steam with a monotonous comparison of notes. To each his own way of relaxation. Sick the man who kept it wholly to himself. Unhappy the one with nothing to do but ruminate in private. There was no time for mourning.

The guns were firing more frequently as ammunition supplies improved. Aircraft were appearing in larger swarms. Another regiment of tanks and then a battery of self-propelled anti-tank guns were entering the minefield gaps, of which three were open and in operation by evening. More and more vehicles and guns dotted the countryside in denser masses. Humanity became subordinated to machinery. The meanest and least articulate gunner, firing in safety from out of sight (and almost out of hearing) could kill the most intellectual person on the enemy side and be quite oblivious to his achievement. The battle's centre of violence shifted south to erode the courage from a shattered protagonist whose machines were in process of being overwhelmed.

Upon these things Irkens and Kramer reflected as they stood under guard and watched the juggernaut roll. They saw a French farmer walking cautiously and sadly in the direction of Vertefeuille Farm. The entitled owners of the land were returning to redoubled toil in the aftermath of the battle.

Yet none of them received more than a passing glance from the General as he drove by, with Arthur Sykes at his side. His eyes were upon the crest, his thoughts up to two moves ahead, planning the battles to come.

26 In Writing

Badgered by Simcox, Dick Tranter sat down at the end of a day of so-called rest to catch up with recording the *Battalion War Diary*. A fortnight had passed since the battle of Vertefeuille Farm, as they now referred to it, and already the clarity of its detail had become blurred. And why not? Fourteen days of unparalleled activity had intervened, and the mere fact that the battalion had been granted this twenty-four hours' respite itself seemed unreal at a time when the tempo of the campaign was gaining in momentum on all sides. Hardly a day had passed when they had not been drawn into a fight. And at last they were breaking free from the *bocage*. Ahead lay the promise of faster and longer advances deeper into the plains of France, making for the River Seine against a German Army which daily, quite distinctly, fought less strongly. To stand aside from the action and pick up his pen to write history when history was being made all around him, demanded a mighty effort. Anyway, he was tired. It would have to be a short account.

'*30 Jul* [he wrote]. Attacked as right-flank protection for the division at 0700 hours and met heavy enemy resistance particularly in vicinity of Vertefeuille Farm. Left-flank company (C) held up for most of day among minefield with heavy losses. Right-flank companies (A followed by B) made steady progress and cleared the final objective shortly before late afternoon to allow remainder of brigade to pass through. Enjoyed useful co-operation with US 301st Battalion on right flank. Placed in reserve 1800 hours but told to move again at 0100 hours, 31 Jul, to support armour held up one mile to south.

'Casualties. Killed: Officers 2, ORs 22. Wounded: Officers 3, ORs 40.'

Harry Spriggs was not much more explicit when he wrote to his wife from hospital a week after his duel with Kramer. A sniper's bullet had gouged his thigh as he led his platoon in a sharp attack against a German ambush near Etouvy. It would heal quickly, they told him. No need for evacuation to England. Since Spriggs was the last to elaborate upon his escapades, his wife, Christine, usually found his letters wonderfully uninformative. It therefore came as a surprise for her to read in some detail about the fight at Vertefeuille – he even named the place – and she guessed that something deeply disturbing had happened there.

'There was this Hun, a big bloke who gave me a fearful scare. We had got into this farm quite easily, though the rest of the company took a knock and you'll be sorry to hear Bill Bateson was killed. They had us taped but I got there ahead of the worst and managed to take some prisoners. Then, as I told you, there was this big bloke who was after my blood and chased me all round what was left of the buildings. I got the blighter in the end. He just came round a corner looking for me, and I drew a bead and then he gave up. It was as easy as that. Seemed a real man. Probably a regular, by the look of him, rather like old RSM Sam Pickering to look at. Had one hell of a row with the Major afterwards which probably did me no end of no good. You know what an old woman he can be and he caught me on the raw after I'd done all the work and he arrived full of orders about something he knew nothing.

'What sort of report did Ethel get at school last term? I thought you might have said in your last but perhaps the post got mixed up . . .'

None of the East Hampshires kept a personal diary and David Garston was a bit of an exception in that he tried to send a commentary to his wife every day. Even this routine, however, had been disrupted by the hectic events after the fight at Vertefeuille Farm and it was 3rd August before he mentioned the adventure and, incidentally, came rather close to breaching the rules of censorship. At the conclusion of his account, compiled from the seat of his jeep during a lull in the fighting, he wrote of people Eileen knew.

'Edward Simcox is an extraordinary fellow. We were all a little doubtful of him in England, as you know. A good company commander but too slow. The hard drinking I thought was a facade and I must say that the first few weeks out here gave one the impression that he was out of his depth commanding the battalion. But since this last battle he has suddenly changed – almost blossomed. In the past forty-eight hours he's been a martinet and given poor Clive Foxton a terrible chasing. Not that Clive hasn't asked for it. Everybody has responded, perhaps in relief as much as anything else. I think we all prefer a firm hand and acknowledge a strong grasp of the man in charge – which Edward certainly failed to demonstrate at first. He'll go wrong if he lets up, of course.

'Strange how the men who were outstanding in England have proved fallible out here and vice versa. Take young Frank Davis. A great man on patrols during schemes but, as I've reason to know, a menace to himself and everybody else with the real thing. Yet brave and determined withall. You should have seen him carry his men forward a few days back. It's the same with the men, too. I would never have thought that a chap like Corporal Parker (you may just remember that he was the one who spilt coffee down your new dress upon which all those clothing coupons had been blown) would have the imagination to lead his section exactly where it was needed. Well, perhaps he does it because he's no imagination. He just keeps going in the direction you point him. In battle who can ask for more than that?

'Truthfully, darling, I find that the most awful thing is recognizing what effect these things have on me, in trying to get the best out of a hundred variegated soldiers. In your practical way you'll say I'm wrong to become too involved. But how can you fail to do so when you see them wilting around you? Make no mistake, we are all wilting. Nobody, so far as I can see, is getting any stronger. We are each, at our own pace, becoming that much less resistant to strain with each extra dose we take. Don't worry about me. I'm indestructible, but some go on for a long time before it's time to stop and some are like shooting stars – they flourish exceedingly and are burnt out in a flash. There was a young man who reached us only a fortnight back. Brave as a lion and intelligent too. In England we would have made him an NCO and picked him for stardom. Suddenly he blew up, reduced to a mental wreck for no clear reason, for I can't believe he saw or heard anything different to the rest of us at the time he broke. I must speak to the Quack about it sometime though God knows when that will be the way things are moving now. Somehow I'd like to survive so that I can tell all this to my children . . .'

The day before Corporal Joe Carter was killed he mailed his aunt the sort of brief message that he had sent her on and off over the years. She had been his confessor in times of need, the one who had spoken wisdom when everybody else failed him. 'I feel, somehow,' he wrote, 'that this war has more to do with us all than most of us out here will admit. The guys in my squad argue about it and don't hit the true reasons. I think because we are all thrown together there's a better knowhow about each other. You begin to see others' points of view and I feel better for it and thank the Army. You know I liked it anyhow. Guess I'll stay on when it's over. That's how I feel now.'

Jurgen Irkens's first letter from captivity to Lotte his wife was more prosaic than normal, as he tried to settle within a totally unfamiliar environment, deeply conscious of the need for caution in the midst of an enemy. Yet contact with the foe seemed to modify his views, as Lotte sensed when she read the note.

'I have been treated well, far better than I would have expected. There is something incongruous about fighting people who are so akin to ourselves. The barriers soon break down despite the hatreds which have been made. I do not even know now if Germany will be victorious, but I pray for you.'

Lotte put it down and crossed the room to close the blackout curtains. The darkness, and with it the night bombers, came much earlier now that winter approached. The future looked bleak and for the first time she felt fear. Nevertheless, from Jurgen's words, she drew just the faintest glimmer of hope.

Lower Chain of Command
In Battle for Vertefeuille Farm.

Legend:
—— PERMANENT COMMAND LINK
- - - SPECIAL LOCAL LINKS

1st.Pentland Yeomanry	1st Bn East Hampshires	P Bty 203rd Fd Regt R.A.	301st U.S. Inf Bn
HQ	HQ	HQ	HQ
A SQN	A COY	FOO	4 COYS
4 TPS	B COY		4 PLS
	C COY		
	3 PLS		

Higher Chain of Command
British Army.

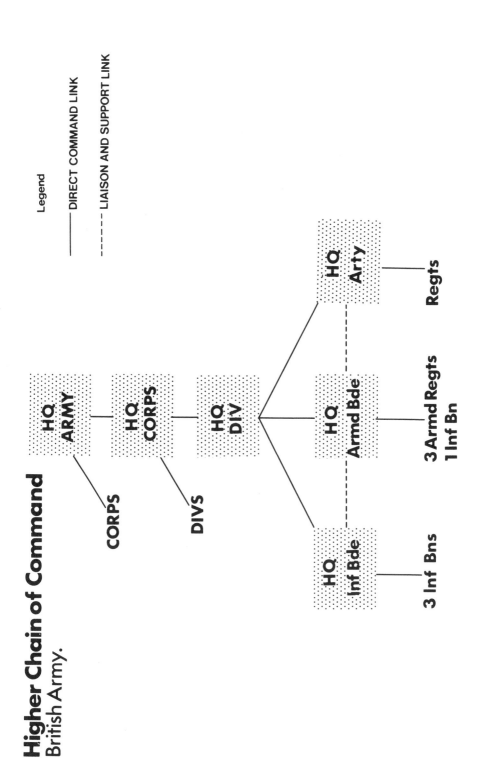

Legend

—— DIRECT COMMAND LINK

------ LIAISON AND SUPPORT LINK

HQ ARMY — CORPS

HQ CORPS — DIVS

HQ DIV

HQ Inf Bde — 3 Inf Bns

HQ Armd Bde — 3 Armd Regts / 1 Inf Bn

HQ Arty — Regts